HOW TO SELL
what you make

HOW TO SELL
what you make
3rd Edition

The Business of Marketing Crafts

Paul Gerhards

STACKPOLE
BOOKS

Published by
STACKPOLE BOOKS
5067 Ritter Road
Mechanicsburg, PA 17055
www.stackpolebooks.com

Printed in the United States of America

10 9 8 7 6 5 4 3 2 1

Cover design by Wendy A. Reynolds

Library of Congress Cataloging-in-Publication Data

Gerhards, Paul.
  How to sell what you make : the business of marketing crafts / Paul Gerhards. — Third edition.
    pages cm
  ISBN 978-0-8117-1139-5 (pbk.)
  1. Selling—Handicraft—Handbooks, manuals, etc. 2. Handicraft—Marketing—Handbooks, manuals, etc. 3. Fairs—Handbooks, manuals, etc. I. Title.
  HF5439.H27G47 2013
  745.5068'8—dc23
                                        2012036222

Contents

Preface

Why, you may ask, would you need a book on marketing and selling crafts when there is already so much free information available on the Internet? It's a good question. The Internet is a great resource. I know, because I use it every day. But in 1988, when I began working on the first edition of *How to Sell What You Make*, the Internet was available only to the government, universities, and other institutions that could afford a supercomputer. Its usefulness to individuals like you and me was nil. The technology and infrastructure to support it were out of reach for the average person. The first Web browser wasn't invented until 1990, the year the first edition of *How to Sell What You Make* was published.

Since then, how we communicate, how we do business, and how we create, market, and sell things have changed—a lot. Even the second edition, which was published in 1996, is filled with references and examples that today are so irrelevant they may as well have been written a hundred years ago. It's about time *How to Sell What You Make* entered the twenty-first century. But the question remains: How can a book on marketing and selling crafts be of any value in the presence of the Internet, where the answers to thousands of questions and heaps of other information are just a click away?

A book is finite and easy to manage, while the Internet is vast and unwieldy. Information contained in this book is limited to its pages, whereas information on the Internet is never-ending.

You won't get lost in the book as you can on the Internet, clicking on link after link. The book is concise and organized in a logical way, but there is nothing organized about the Internet, and there is no logic to it either.

How to Sell What You Make is written for people who want to know more about what's necessary to get into the crafts business, including marketing, selling, and the day-to-day clerical aspects of running a business. After you've read the book, you'll want to use it as a point of departure to find specific and up-to-date information about shows and fairs you can attend and investigate topics specific to your needs. That's what the Internet is for.

chapter 1

Crafts as a Business: An Introduction

Are you among the many talented and creative people who aspire to make a living off things crafted by your own hands? Are you one of those innovative people who design and make beautiful objects but sometimes wonder what to do with them once they are finished? Did you spend years studying your craft and now want more from your labor than just a way to pass the time?

When you think of yourself as a crafter, what's the first thing that comes to mind? Maybe you see yourself as a creator of objects of utilitarian or aesthetic value, or both. Perhaps you consider yourself an artist or a holder of fundamental secrets to your craft that you have acquired through diligence and dedication. Your work—the job that you do—is an outlet for your passion. You did not just stumble into your job. You *created* it. You are your own boss, with all the duties and responsibilities that go with the position.

For most of us in the crafts business, being your own boss means there is no authority to report to. You are accountable to no one but yourself. You don't have to call in sick, and you can be late to work if you want to. But it's not that simple. Crafts making is a *business*. No more, no less. It's up to you and you alone to make and grow your business to the level to which you are capable of taking it. As sole proprietor, you hold several positions. It's not enough to be a skilled artisan. You must also be good at marketing and sales, bookkeeping and accounting, fulfillment and customer service.

You are the manufacturer of a marketable product. Put aside for a moment the associations the word *manufacture* has with factories and assembly lines, employees and unions, department stores and shopping malls. *Manufacture* is just another word for *make*.

What differentiates making crafts from ordinary manufacturing is how you do it. This doesn't necessarily mean that you do it all yourself and by hand with Old World tools; rather, it refers to your connectedness with the design, the materials, and the people you work with. This connectedness is fundamental to crafts and craftsmanship.

When you last purchased something from a big-box store—an appliance, say—did you feel a connectedness with the worker on the line who turned nut A onto bolt B? Among all the multilingual manuals and instructions, did you get a brochure describing how the product was made and by whom? Probably not. Perhaps you have seen labels reading, "Union Made in the USA." Regardless of the national and class pride the phrase evokes, it's more a sociopolitical statement than a personal one. This is not meant to diminish the value of unions or an individual union member's pride in his or her work, whatever the job may be. But the larger the organizational structure, the less connection there is between the individual and the product. Things are manufactured not by individuals, but by companies that employ people who work in factories, often overseas.

"Handcrafted in America" means someone *created* the object. The piece has roots. It is the crafter's duty to the industry, then, to cultivate and protect that connection that keeps the roots strong and productive. As a manufacturer of handcrafted items, you have a wonderful opportunity to perpetuate a tradition, not only of crafts and creativity, but also of personal and honest relationships in business.

When you begin thinking of turning your skills into a business, you enter into an industry that has been growing steadily for the past fifty years. As an industry, crafts came into their own during the 1960s with a resurgence in interest in handcrafted items. Makers of contemporary crafts came to appreciate the value of making things by hand, and consumers saw the value in owning things so produced.

Handicrafts were every bit a facet of the back-to-the-land movement, which spawned a search for roots and a connectedness with things natural. It continues with the desire of many talented people to live "off the grid" but within a culture of individuality. The catchphrase "high-tech versus high-touch" merely gives a new dimension to an older philosophy. Technology continues to solve problems (as well as create new ones) for an ever more complex society. But technology has a sterile nature, a coldness many of us can't get close to. Even with all the emphasis on social networking, one is still at a distance, being social alone. Working within the crafts industry is a way of keeping in touch with our humanity.

For many crafters, the first step in selling crafts is the local crafts fair. Some fairs are held weekly; others are annual events, often in conjunction with regional celebrations. Crafts fairs are relatively easy and inexpensive to get into and offer a number of opportunities for both novice and veteran crafters. The most important opportunity is in the sheer volume of people attracted to crafts fairs and markets. They are wonderful places to meet the buying public and fellow crafters and to learn what is selling this year and what isn't.

Selling directly to local shops and galleries is another way crafters market their wares. Just about every town or city has at least one crafts outlet, and taking the direct approach has many advantages over selling at fairs.

Another marketplace, one where people come for the sole purpose of buying, and buying in quantity, is the crafts trade show. Nearly every industry has at least one trade show each year, and the crafts industry is no exception. Crafts trade shows are where shop and gallery owners or representatives come to you to buy your crafts to stock their shelves.

A trade show is not necessarily a better way to sell crafts, nor are people who exhibit at one better crafters than those who don't. It is merely one of several marketing strategies available to enterprising crafters. But it is a sophisticated approach to selling crafts. It demands a high degree of professionalism.

The crafts business is a demanding one, and the industry is highly competitive. Competition has infused the industry with ever-higher standards of professionalism. For the crafter, this means learning a new set of skills and gaining a thorough understanding of both the crafts business and general business principles. Professionalism and high standards don't guarantee success, but you are more likely to support yourself with them than without them.

Crafts making is a culture and a lifestyle. Crafts selling is a business. The successful crafter integrates both. Most small businesses fail because of a lack of capital and poor management skills. To succeed in the crafts business, the crafter must acquire more than just a dash of business acumen. Do not, however, confuse success with dollars. Define what success means to you, and then strive for it. The goal is earning a living, and all goals require sacrifice.

One such sacrifice is to shed the wardrobe and attitude of "starving artist" and replace them with those of a more entrepreneurial nature. This does not mean selling out to the system or replacing your apron with a three-piece suit. What it does mean is learning what it takes to run a business and how to do it well. Creativity, and the pride it engenders, remains intact.

The crafts industry exists because it satisfies many of the wants and needs of consumers. Without demand, there would be no crafts industry, at least on the scale it has achieved. The same holds true for an individual crafts business. It justifies its existence by satisfying the wants and needs of a portion of society through its products or services. A crafts business for its own sake ceases to be a business and becomes a hobby, fulfilling only the wants and needs of the crafter. One goal is no more or less noble than the other, but understanding the difference between the two is essential for success.

Terms and Distinctions

Like any industry, the crafts industry has its own jargon. Words, phrases, and concepts understood automatically by those involved sometimes sound confusing or ambiguous to the novice or casual observer of the trade. Some terms are interchangeable, and others have specific meanings. Still others are cause for dispute among the players.

One of the most challenging areas to broach is that of crafts itself. Because the field of crafts is so diverse, it is often difficult to draw, let alone recognize, boundaries among the many categories. It is important to understand that there are differences, because in some cases these differences impose limitations on which shows, fairs, and other events you can attend.

The word *craft* has broad applications. It can mean skill and dexterity in accomplishing certain tasks. In the crafts industry, it is understood that merchandise is made largely by hand with skill and dexterity.

It becomes tricky when some handcrafted items—items that for all intents and purposes are genuinely crafts—are excluded from certain arenas. Take for example the woman who makes Christmas wreaths but was not selected to exhibit in a certain trade show. Why? The promoter did not consider wreath making a craft. The promoter sets standards, guidelines, and limits, and what one considers crafts are not necessarily considered crafts by another.

Wreath making is better classified as *country crafts* or *folk art*, and there are several shows where wreaths would be welcome. A country craft is no less a craft than, say, fine jewelry making, when undertaken with skill and dexterity, but the distinction should be obvious. It is necessary for the crafter to determine in which market his or her handiwork would be most accepted.

High-end and *low-end* are two concepts used to further distinguish crafts. High-end refers to crafts produced with the highest standards of quality and design. As such, they also demand the highest prices. Low-end describes those crafts at the opposite extreme. This is not to suggest that all low-end crafts are shoddily made and their design ill considered. High-end also refers to the relative uniqueness of the item, as well as the degree of professionalism with which it is displayed. Even low-end crafts have high-end and low-end components.

One distinguishing factor between high-end and low-end may also be used to distinguish between *art* and *craft*. An art piece is distinctly one of a kind, but a craft is something replicable, not only by the original maker, but also by others.

No one person can make an objective, sweeping judgment of what is low-end and high-end. Quality is often subjective, and it is up to you to determine where you and your work fit in. As a test, visit a few crafts fairs and judge for yourself.

Fairs, trade shows, and *gift shows* are nebulous and sometimes overlapping terms. *Crafts fair* usually refers to a retail event, which is open to the public. Sometimes they are held in conjunction with local or regional celebrations; other times they are held in their own right. A *trade show,* as a rule, is open only to members of the crafts trade—that is, businesses that buy from you at *wholesale* price points but sell your work at *retail.* (See chapter 9 for discussion of wholesale and retail pricing.) Some trade shows have both wholesale and retail days, the latter being open to the public.

Another distinction to make is between crafts fairs and *crafts shows.* Typically, anyone can have a booth at a fair, but shows, which are open to the public, are *juried.* In a juried show, your work is judged for its appropriateness. You'll find more on the jury system in chapter 4.

A *gift show* is a trade show that caters to the gift trade and therefore has a focus far different from that of the crafts trade. Crafts make excellent gifts, and that's why many crafters exhibit at gift shows. However, many items at gift shows were mass-produced abroad and imported and distributed by large companies.

Many trade shows outside of the crafts trade welcome crafters. Exploring such avenues as fashion and accessories, architectural design, interior decorating, and office supply is encouraged, provided your work is appropriate for the event. Each of these is a new frontier for crafters who have products that fill a niche.

Retail outlets also have distinctions. A *gift shop* stocks its shelves with gifts much like any other store stocks its shelves with its specific kinds of merchandise. A *crafts gallery,* on the other hand, tends to exhibit crafts in groupings of work by individual crafters.

The *crafts mall* is another opportunity for some crafters. Typically, a crafts mall is a large store that is divided into small spaces that are rented or leased to crafters. Crafters do not have to be in attendance during business hours, because mall owners or managers handle sales for them.

Show (or fair) promoter and *show management* are synonymous. The promoter is the person or persons, under the auspices of a corporation, responsible for the show and all of its aspects from advertising the show to booking an arena. *Facilities management* is the governing body of the building or buildings where the trade show is held. The promoter deals with facilities management, but each exhibitor is responsible for following any established house rules.

The promoter's job is to bring crafters and buyers together for their mutual benefit. Therefore, the promoter must see to the wants and needs of both parties to ensure a successful show. One way this happens is that the promoter strives to make available for buyers a wide range of products and *price points*—industry jargon for price.

One of a kind, as the term implies, refers to individual craft items, each one unique. These pieces usually demand higher prices because of their uniqueness. Although any two items made entirely by hand are unique by varying degrees, one of a kind refers here to something that is unique in design and execution, something that cannot or will not be exactly duplicated. It does not refer to, say, ceramic plates that, because of the vagaries of the glazing process, come from the kiln different from all the others. *Production crafts*, or *multiples*, are mass-produced items.

The terms *booth*, *display*, and *exhibit* are sometimes used interchangeably, although technically they are different. The *booth space* is what you occupy at a show or fair. Larger indoor shows demarcate booth space with pipe and drape or another kind of partition. Smaller indoor shows may not. Outdoors, space may be marked off in various ways or even verbally, as in, "Somewhere over there." In either setting, inside or out, you can construct a freestanding enclosure, a *booth*, as a setting in which you display your wares.

Your *display* is what you show, including your method of presentation. *Exhibit* takes display a step further. An exhibit generally shows and tells. For example, a series of photographs and text—or actual step-by-step models—depicting how you make your wares is an exhibit.

Marketing and *selling* are terms sometimes used interchangeably, but there are big differences between the two. *Selling* is the act of exchanging your goods for cash. *Marketing* is an all-encompassing concept that includes research, advertising, and communicating with potential buyers. Those potential and actual buyers are your *market*. Read about creating a *business plan* (which includes a *marketing plan*) in chapter 9.

This book is not about how to get rich selling crafts. Its purpose, rather, is to do the following:

- provide an overview of how to sell crafts at fairs and shows and in shops and galleries;
- teach you how to apply to and prepare for fairs and trade shows;
- prepare you for what you can expect when you get there;
- demonstrate how you can apply generally accepted sales methods to any event; and
- give modest instruction on how to apply standard business practices to your crafts enterprise.

Whether you consider yourself a crafter, designer, craftsman, artisan, artist, or crafts maker, if you can create fine-quality handcrafted items, you likely can sell them. This book introduces you, the crafter with something to sell, to the many ways to market and sell what you make.

chapter 2

Crafts Fairs and Street Fairs: Your Direct Link to Consumers

In days gone by, many crafters were nomads. Cobblers, coopers, tinkers, smiths, and others traveled the countryside plying their trades, exchanging goods and services for hard cash or a hearty meal. Towns and villages had open-air markets where they could hawk their wares. Today crafters cling to their nomadic roots as they travel from town to town, crafts fair to crafts fair, setting up and tearing down—all to sell what they make. Neither the forum nor the purpose has changed much over the years, despite rapid changes in technology.

Crafts fairs run the gamut of sizes from small-town events that serve as backdrops for celebrations to expansive affairs in major cities. These retail fairs offer something for everyone. Unless your town has a permanent or semipermanent crafts marketplace where you can establish an ongoing presence, travel—and lots of it—is required to operate successfully on the crafts fair circuit.

Success on the retail circuit requires planning and organization. The more fairs you attend yearly, the more important scheduling becomes. Application deadlines must be met, booth fees or deposits paid, travel arrangements made. And it's ever so important to attend the right fairs. Research into fairs saves time and money by helping you avoid unproductive events or ones not suited to your business. How widely advertised is the fair? What is the expected attendance? Is it held outdoors, in a tent, or within a permanent building? What is the caliber of crafts exhibited? Is the fair held for its own sake or is it just one of many attractions of a larger event? How many exhibitors are expected? Is the fair open or juried? What is the fair's sales track record? A little research on the Internet will be invaluable to you for the answers it will bring. And the Internet is one place where belonging to and participating in social networks like Facebook will yield a rich harvest of answers to perplexing questions.

Salesmanship at the Street Level

Good sales techniques can mean the difference between success and failure at any fair. Retailing at crafts fairs involves meeting and greeting people. The more people you meet and greet, the more opportunities you have for sales. The inexperienced or introverted exhibitor waits for potential buyers to express interest in buying. Crafters experienced in retailing attract buyers in any number of ways, both subtle and obvious. There is no need for hard-sell tactics. A simple smile and a friendly greeting may be all it takes to convert a browser to a buyer. But it may take more than that. Talk about your products. Encourage fairgoers to handle your crafts. Explain how you make them, how they can be used. If you have something whose use can be demonstrated, then do so regularly. That draws attention. Can you work on your crafts in your booth? This, too, attracts crowds. Pay close attention to those who stop by your booth more than once. Chances are they are trying to make a decision. Do what you can to encourage a decision in your favor. Anything you can do to engage someone is to your benefit.

One of the most important elements of your crafts fair business is your booth (see chapter 8). Your booth is your storefront. It must reflect you and your work in the most positive of manners. It must be rugged enough to withstand the rigors of the circuit and highly portable for easy transport and setup. It must also, if necessary, be able to protect you and your work from the elements.

Advantages of Selling at Crafts Fairs

Crafts fairs are relatively easy to get into. Therefore, they offer a great opportunity to get your work before the public. This is an important step for any crafter. Street fairs and markets are great places to test new ideas and experiment with prices (see chapter 9). Trends often change as rapidly as the weather, and it's important to know what's popular and what isn't. The crafter with stale ideas and dime-a-dozen products won't do as well as the one with fresh and invigorating designs and products that speak for themselves.

Retail events serve as the link between you and crafts consumers. Talk with them. Find out what they like and dislike. Learning what the public wants and what it will buy—and providing it to them—is the margin between success and failure.

Disadvantages of Selling at Crafts Fairs

A big disadvantage to regularly selling at crafts fairs is the amount of time you must spend on the road and away from your shop or studio. Nearly every weekend of the year involves travel, setup, and selling. As a circuit-riding crafter, you have to strike a constant balance between producing and marketing.

The challenge is to have enough goods on hand to display and sell one weekend and still have time to replenish your stock.

Travel is hard work in itself, and not everyone is suited to the discipline it entails. If you have a family that accompanies you, especially one with young children, the regimen can be grueling for everyone.

Another drawback is in the nature of the fairs themselves. In many cases, they are an adjunct to a greater event—a community celebration, for example. And even if they are independent events, they possess a large degree of entertainment value. More people may come just for the fun of it rather than to buy anything. You may spend some weekends smiling politely as crowds walk by without much more than a nod in your direction.

Taking Cash

Of course, you'll want to take in lots of cash. And that means you'll need to take a lot of cash with you to make change. Plan on having at least $50 in ones and fives, and $10 in coins to start out with. After a couple of shows, you'll have a better idea of your needs. A good cash box will help keep things sorted. Be sure you keep it out of arm's reach of passersby in busy crowds. Some crafters prefer a waist pack to a cash box. It's always with you, but it makes it more difficult to keep bills and change sorted out. Whatever method you use, have an accurate count of your cash on hand at the beginning of the event. Subtract the opening balance from the final count to know your cash sales for the day.

Some people are more fastidious in their accounting practices than others, but it's a good idea to keep track of every sale by writing a receipt, even if the customer doesn't want a copy, or by keeping a running tally. At the end of the day, you'll know just how you did in sales. Be sure to include credit card sales (discussed next) as part of your take for the day. Don't forget to account for cash taken out for coffee, lunch, or other expenses. Look for any discrepancies. If there are discrepancies greater than, say, $10, you'll want to know why. If you're working a weekend event, at the end of each day, remove the day's take—and deposit it, if you can—and start the next morning with your initial bank of cash in the box.

Taking Credit Card Payments

There was a time when taking credit payments required a special merchant account with monthly fees attached, in addition to the transaction fees. You needed either an expensive card reader with a dedicated phone line—which was impossible, if not impractical, to acquire at the average crafts fair—or an inexpensive imprinter. Using an imprinter required that you input the card information at the end of the day. This tedious activity demanded accuracy. Also, higher transaction fees were likely assessed for manual data entry. So in the past, taking credit or debit card payments was not cost-effective for the sole proprietor working on a tight budget. Transactions were made with either cash or check.

Today many people prefer not to carry cash and instead make all their purchases with a credit or debit card. When you are forced to say, "Sorry, cash or check only," because you're not equipped to take card payments, this could mean the difference between a good sales day and a bad one.

Fortunately, taking credit card or debit card payments at events is easier—and less expensive—than ever, provided you have a smartphone or tablet device with cellular access. Assuming you *do* have one of these, you can sign up for one or more of several payment systems that allow you to take credit or debit payments by running the card through a free reader (along with a free application) attached to your device. You will still pay transaction fees—approximately 3 percent—as a cost of doing business. See the appendix for information about merchant accounts and other payment systems.

chapter 3

The Gallery Connection: Stepping into the Wholesale Marketplace

S hop and gallery owners need merchandise to sell. It's how they make their living. They buy their merchandise at a discount—that is, wholesale—from the manufacturer and then sell it at retail, the price the consumer pays.

Crafters who understand that shop owners need what they have—crafts—also understand that they offer a service by providing merchandise to dealers. By making your crafts and services available to those who will buy from you and sell it to others, you foster business relationships that last a long time. But you have to meet them first.

The worst way to approach a shop owner is by knocking on the front door unannounced, towing a wagonload of goods. The proprietor may be busy, unavailable, or have personal protocols that must be followed, and time and effort will be wasted on both sides of the sales counter. Once again, preparation, planning, and organization make the difference between amateur and professional behavior.

There is no one best way of approaching a shop or gallery. Some general guidelines may help, though. Always make an appointment with the person who has the authority to purchase your work or place an order. Dealing with seconds in command is of no value unless they have decision-making, contract-signing, and check-writing power.

Matters of Formality

The most formal way of approaching a gallery or shop is to prepare and mail an introductory packet. This consists of a cover letter, résumé, sales literature, and photographs of your work (see chapter 5). The purpose of the cover letter is twofold: to introduce you and to indicate a degree of professionalism. The cover letter, printed on your business letterhead, should be short and to the point—not more than a page. Address it to the person with whom you eventually will do business, not "to whom it may concern." If you don't know whom it concerns, find out. A phone call should do the job.

Explain in the cover letter that you are interested in placing your work in the prospective buyer's store and why. The *why* is for the owner's benefit, not yours (see chapter 5). Summarize your qualifications, saving the details for your résumé. Tell the buyer you would like to make an appointment to further discuss doing business in, say, two weeks' time, and that you will be phoning soon to make the arrangements. Then list the other materials enclosed in the packet; for example, "For your consideration, I've enclosed my résumé, photographs of my work, sales literature, and a wholesale price list." If you want any of the materials returned, such as your photographs, say so near the end of the letter. Then make it easy for the buyer by enclosing a self-addressed, stamped envelope. As a matter of professional courtesy, this is a must. It also places the onus of response on the buyer. It opens the door for the buyer to send you a brief note of interest or lack thereof.

Make the résumé as brief but as complete as possible, one page at the most. It doesn't necessarily have to be the same kind of résumé you would use in applying for a job. Nor is it your life story. It should simply be an outline of your qualifications. List only those qualifications pertaining to your craft. That you have a degree in fine arts is one thing. Information such as that you have only a high school education but have served six years on the local school board and coach a youth soccer team is of little relevance to the situation. Be sure to list any awards received for your crafts, affiliations with crafts organizations, trade shows attended, and how long you've been practicing your craft.

A week or so after you mail your packet, keep your promise and follow up with a phone call to arrange an appointment. Then take along as many samples and sales aids as you think you need to influence a decision in your favor. Sales aids may include appropriate display cases or racks and literature—anything that will make your crafts more attractive to the consumer.

A less formal, and less expensive, approach is to send the buyer a brief email with a link to your website.

Selling on Approval

Naturally, what you're after is setting up a wholesale account, where the shop owner places an order and pays cash on delivery, or within a specified amount of time. If the owner declines to purchase your crafts outright, the next resort is to offer them on approval, an alternative to selling on consignment (discussed in the next section).

The simplicity of the on-approval arrangement, as compared with the complexity of consignment, makes it attractive to the buyer. When selling on approval, you present the buyer a line of products and sales aids to display for a limited time, perhaps ten to thirty days but no more than sixty. At the end of that period, the shop owner has two options: purchase the entire package at full wholesale value or return the merchandise, paying only for those pieces, if any, that were sold. You may be expected to pay shipping charges for the returns. Be sure to include return shipping terms in the agreement.

The financial risk for the buyer during this trial period is nil. And the risk to you is minimal. Your willingness to trust the gallery with your crafts indicates a degree of sincerity and professionalism. What's more, if your crafts benefit the store in sales, there is no reason for the owner not to purchase the trial products and place orders for more under the standard wholesale arrangement. Even with established accounts, shipping a few *new*, but unordered, products on approval along with an order is an excellent way to test the market. If you do so, enclose a note explaining why you've included items that weren't ordered and saying that the owner can return them if they don't sell.

The limited period established in the on-approval agreement benefits both parties. For you, it's an opportunity to test a market without tying up merchandise indefinitely. If sales don't occur, try to determine why. Was your merchandise displayed prominently? If the answer is no, the owner didn't invest the energy and resources, and chances are your products would not have received better treatment had they been purchased outright. If the answer is yes, chances are the clientele was not a good match for your crafts. For the gallery owner, a specified period is an opportunity to determine whether the clientele is receptive to your crafts without indefinitely tying up valuable shelf space. If the match is not a good one, you part company. If nothing else, you've learned a bit more about the market.

Regardless of the outcome, the terms of the on-approval agreement must be spelled out in writing before the merchandise is placed to eliminate any cause for misunderstanding between the parties. The on-approval agreement should include these points:

- description and quantity of items
- wholesale price
- duration of agreement
- liability for loss or damage
- end-of-agreement terms (purchase of entire lot or payment for pieces sold and return of unsold pieces)

Selling on Consignment

Selling on consignment is a long-standing tradition in the crafts business. Its advantages lean heavily in favor of the shop owner, but even then, they are often offset by an increase in paperwork and accounting. The advantages to the crafter are few, but they, too, have their offsetting factors.

In consignment selling, the crafter places merchandise in the care of the shop owner with no guarantee of sale. The crafter is the sole owner of the property until purchased by the consumer. The shop has no monetary investment in the merchandise at any time. In effect, the crafter is lending merchandise to the shop owner. But ownership may not always be as apparent as it would seem.

The Universal Commercial Code, put into effect in the 1950s to establish and maintain uniform business standards among the states, gives some protection to artists and craftspeople. However, if the shop goes into bankruptcy, creditors may include and go after *your* merchandise with the rest of the shop's inventory to help recoup their losses. Specifically and officially assigning ownership is one of many reasons a solid written contract needs to be drawn between you and the shop or gallery.

For the unestablished crafter with untried items, consignment may be the only way to get merchandise into a shop. Additionally, upon sale of an item, crafters may realize a higher monetary return than they would by selling at wholesale. Whereas the wholesale return is customarily 50 percent of the retail price, standard consignment returns may run from 60 to 70 percent.

In many cases, however, the extra percentage points may be false profits. For example, if you sell ten pieces up front to the store at a wholesale price of $10 each, you take home $100 regardless of whether the pieces are later sold at retail. If you place the same ten pieces on consignment at 70 percent of the retail price of $20, you have a potential total return of $140. But suppose only five of the pieces sell and the rest are returned damaged or shopworn. Your financial return is but $70 on the five; the others represent a total wholesale loss of $50, leaving you with just $20 spread over the ten items. Clearly, selling on consignment is a gamble.

For the shop owner, taking crafts on consignment is an opportunity to stock shelves without investing financially in the merchandise. But the owner pays for that privilege in higher costs: 70 percent of the retail price goes to the crafter rather than 50 percent, meaning less profit if a sale is made. On the other hand, if a sale is not made, the absence of investment means no loss. Reversing the above example illustrates the point. A wholesale purchase of the ten pieces represents $100 in costs to the shop owner. If all ten pieces are sold at $20 each, retail, the owner realizes a gross return of $200, half of which pays the cost of purchase, leaving $100 in profit. (This is not all profit, however, because much of the $100 could go to cover operating costs.) If all ten pieces were sold on consignment, then the shop owner would receive in return just $60, or 30 percent of the combined retail price of $200. Just five pieces sold would net the retailer $30, but he would not have to absorb the $50 wholesale cost of the remaining five. Accepting crafts on consignment is safer than outright purchase, but that safety comes at a price.

An intangible cost to the shop owner who takes part in a consignment agreement is added paperwork. Once merchandise owned by the retailer is sold, it is money in the cash register. A consignment sale is something different altogether. When a consigned item is sold to the public, the retailer then must buy it, as it were, from the crafter after the fact. This means that the retailer must record and follow up on each sale with a check, either after the sale is made or according to a prearranged schedule, such as monthly or quarterly.

Two prevailing reasons a shop owner will take crafts on consignment are a lack of capital and little faith in the marketability of the crafts in question. What would you, the crafter, think of a business that was so low on capital that it couldn't purchase its stock? When you turn over crafts on consignment, essentially you are making an unsecured loan to the store with the hope of a high return. If lack of capital is indeed the problem, then it's a good guess that cash flow also is a problem. And this could spell problems for you. What if two or three of your pieces sell today, and the rent on the store is due tomorrow? The question is rhetorical, because no one can know the mind of the person who has to pay the rent and the crafter but hasn't the money for both.

If the shop owner has little faith in the marketability of your work, then he or she will make little or no effort to sell it aggressively. You'd be better off looking for another outlet with better terms.

Expensive, high-end, one-of-a-kind items are the exception to the above examples and must be mentioned in defense of honorable retailers who handle such merchandise. These items, by their very nature, aren't highly marketable and can certainly place a financial burden on the gallery owner.

Any consignment agreement should contain the following:

- description and quantity of each product
- retail price and percentage to both consignee (retailer) *and* consignor (you)
- hidden costs to you (e.g., credit card fees if customers purchase your items with a card, prorated share of utilities and rent, and so on)
- duration of consignment
- method of payment (monthly or immediately upon sale)
- liability for loss or damage (inquire whether the store's insurance policy covers consigned items)
- who pays shipping charges for returns
- statement of ownership (in case of bankruptcy)
- exclusivity

Crafts Malls

In the crafts mall setting, individual crafters lease or rent display space within a larger store or group of stores. Your work may be juried for selection. Once granted a space, you are free to display your wares in any manner acceptable to the mall owner or manager.

Just as with consignment and on-approval selling, you are not required to attend your wares; the mall's personnel take care of sales for you. But you are required to pay rent regardless of sales.

Before signing a lease agreement, ask other crafters about their success in the mall. Find out if the mall is in a high-traffic area and whether the other crafters make enough money from sales to at least cover their rent each month. Also ask about rent stability: has the rent remained constant or has it been going progressively upward? Are there any hidden fees aside from rent? Another important consideration is whether the owners carry theft and fire insurance.

chapter 4

Selling to the Trade: Expanding Your Market

When you sell crafts at a retail fair, you bring your work into the local marketplace. Your potential customers are local and may be attracted to the event for a variety of reasons. The marketplace is diverse and defined only by its geographic area. You rely largely on the impulses of the visitors.

At the crafts fair, once you've made a sale, your relationship with the individual buyer is over, at least for the moment. It's true that word-of-mouth advertising could bring others to your booth. It's equally true that some buyers may return for additional pieces of your work—if you are there at a later fair date, whether it's the next day, week, or year. But as a rule, you deal one-on-one with the buying public, and each sale is a one-time-only event.

When you sell directly to shops and galleries, whether at wholesale, on consignment, or on approval, you enter a more specific marketplace. Your dealers, or potential dealers, have defined that marketplace for you through their clientele. When they accept your work, they have a good reason for doing so: they believe it will sell and therefore will add to their income.

But unless you have one or more sales representatives (see chapter 7), visiting all the potential outlets across the country would be an impossible chore.

Exhibiting at one or more trade shows can give you and your products valuable exposure to hundreds of serious buyers now and prospective buyers later on. At the trade show, you deal one-on-one with representatives of many blocs of consumers, and you are likely to establish ongoing business relationships with people outside your geographic area. This is the advantage of trade-show marketing: you have the ability to reach many through few.

How Trade Shows Differ from Retail Events

One of the first things a novice will notice when considering exhibiting at a trade show is the cost. It takes a significant investment of time and money. Aside from booth fees, which can be as much as $2,250 for a ten-by-ten-foot booth, there are other costs associated with exhibiting: travel and shipping, food and lodging, parking and recreation.

A major distinction between shows that cater to the crafts trade and shows that cater to the public is pricing. A trade show is a wholesale show, where you sell at a price much lower than the consumer ultimately pays.

Crafters without adequate pricing experience find it difficult to cut their prices by half—the industry standard—to sell to trade buyers. Many novices to the crafts business do not recognize that they essentially are operating two businesses at the same time: a wholesale business and a retail business. The danger lies in treating these businesses as one, without realizing that each virtually distinct business has separate and distinct costs of operation (see chapter 9). Each business profile, wholesale and retail, arrives at its price points much as any other business would: costs plus a little profit added on. Because their retail-business costs inadvertently are lumped together with wholesale-business costs, crafters selling at the retail level are likely to set prices somewhere between true wholesale and true retail. The consumer gets a bargain.

Unfortunately, retail merchants (shops and galleries) and crafters who wholesale exclusively are hurt by this practice, because they can't adequately compete with prices set in such an arbitrary manner. The professional crafter who wholesales recognizes that, in theory as well as practice, retail prices aren't cut by half to sell to trade buyers; rather, wholesale prices are doubled to sell to consumers.

If crafters could sell directly to all of the potential retail buyers that could be reached via trade buyers (shop and gallery owners), there would be little use for trade shows. Indeed, many professional crafters operate their own galleries or shops, and their prices reflect both wholesale and retail costs. But many of them also rely on trade shows to expose their wares to a much wider consumer base. Essentially, those retail dollars that could be gained by selling directly to the public is the price they pay for that exposure. But they are nondollars because, chances are, the crafter would not have reached those buyers in the first place. What's important is that wholesale prices be at a point that yields a comfortable profit and an acceptable standard of living for both wholesaler and retailer.

Since the price points you offer on an item can have an impact on the entire industry, strive to keep your retail prices competitive. If you have a wholesale account in the same area as a fair you attend, don't undercut the gallery's prices. Undercutting jeopardizes the account and puts you in competition with yourself. A better idea is to tell buyers where they can order more of your crafts locally. This free advertising for the gallery shows much goodwill on your part.

Another big difference between selling at trade shows and selling at retail fairs is production scheduling. Because trade-show buyers place orders for products instead of buying existing stock outright, production schedules are based on orders written at the show or soon thereafter, with the exception that some existing stock may be available to meet early delivery deadlines. Trade-show exhibitors take with them samples of their work to show prospective buyers. Retail circuit riders take with them a sizable portion of their inventory to sell to prospective buyers. Maybe they will sell out, which is good. But maybe they will take most of it back. In any case, production schedules and output are based on upcoming retail events rather than past wholesale events.

The objective of the trade show is to show buyers what you make and how well you make it. If they like what they see and believe they can sell it, they will place orders. The buyers go away with the prospect of soon acquiring your quality crafts for their stores; you go away with the prospect of enough work to keep you busy, happy, and well fed for months to come.

So who exactly are crafts trade shows for—the maker or the buyer? The answer is both. There is a symbiotic relationship between the two, just as in any buying-selling relationship. The shop owner cannot exist without things to sell, nor can you, the crafter, exist (presuming a desire to exist on crafts) without people to buy your handiwork, and lots of it.

The competitive atmosphere of crafts trade shows imposes high professional standards on crafters. These standards have both positive and negative effects on the industry. On the positive side, they promote quality in craftsmanship and help satisfy a large-scale demand for quality crafts. The negative effects are subtler. Some crafters fear that too much emphasis on competition and professionalism precludes innovation and stifles creativity. This is especially true when crafters become merely producers and sellers of the same things year after year just because certain crafts are profitable. Crafters who cease to be innovative for the sake of profit often find themselves suddenly standing still in a changing market.

You can overcome this complacency, however, by fostering diligence and a desire to push your creative and artistic abilities to the limit.

What Trade Shows Can Do for Your Business

Attending one or more trade shows each year can do a number of things for your business. The trade show is a wide and varied network where veterans and novices can gain new insights into the industry and gather information about it. It's a place where you can get concentrated lessons on how to improve your marketing and selling skills.

The trade show puts you at the center of a network of people who work in your field and in the crafts community as a whole, where you will learn more about the craft trade and market trends. Networking has become a common and valuable way of exchanging information. When you find yourself in a group of people who share common interests and goals, as well as common problems and frustrations, you also find a dynamism that cannot exist in isolation. Ideas and solutions not only are exchanged, they are created spontaneously when like-minded people interact. Within the crafts community, you'll find camaraderie and crafters who are willing to share the knowledge they gained through experience.

Buyers, too, are a part of the network. Because buyers deal directly with consumers who live all over the country, they have a keen understanding of the market. They have a sense of where the market is going and how it is traveling. Trade buyers are a valuable source of information about trends and what may or may not work in the marketplace. Do you have an idea about a new product and wonder whether the market is ready for it? Ask a buyer familiar with the craft. Is one of your products not moving as well as you'd like? Ask the opinion of people who are not buying.

A third component in the network is the trade-show promoter. The promoter sets the stage for buyer and seller to meet and do business. As a secondary function, some promoters serve as educators. They publish newsletters and other literature filled with helpful advice on all phases of the business. Also available through show management are seminars and workshops addressing specific issues related to the trade. Promoters are motivated by the desire to enable buyer and seller to succeed, for without their success, the reputation of the show is compromised and attendance dwindles.

Trade shows can help you sharpen your marketing and selling skills. Marketing and selling are not synonymous, and understanding their difference is crucial to any business. Marketing has to do with reaching customers—the people who buy crafts, the people who either like or don't like what you have. Selling deals with products. To whom you sell—that is, your targeted market—is based on information gathered through the marketing process. There are any number of good books on marketing, the hows and wherefores of selling, but as always, experience is the best teacher. And it's through experience that you learn the finer nuances between marketing and selling.

Finally, a trade show can give your business the financial boost it needs. Millions of dollars' worth of orders are written at each major show. Though some crafts categories fare better than others, as do some individual crafts, the distribution of business is across the board. The crafter prepared to enter the world of crafts trade shows can expect to share in the rewards of the national marketplace.

Don't expect all this to happen during your first show, however. There is nothing wrong with great expectations, but any expectation has to be kept in perspective. All businesses take time to develop. The trade show is not a magic solution for marketing and selling; rather, it's one of several opportunities. Dozens of variables are involved. Some of them you have control over, others you don't. Perhaps the biggest obstacle is getting into the show—or shows—of your choice in the first place. Each show has a limited number of booths, and hundreds of people want one. You may not get into the first trade show you apply for, and if you do get into a show, you may not get selected to exhibit in the same show the following year. But if you are persistent, just as there is a market for your crafts, so too is there a booth from which you can sell them.

Because of the investment of time and money, take care to select a show that attracts buyers interested in what you have. The character and atmosphere of each show is different, and you must be as scrupulous as possible in your selection. It's just another part of doing business. You wouldn't try to sell quilts in a pottery gallery or one-of-a-kind furniture in an airport gift shop. A first show takes an enormous amount of optimism to get through, but going in with little more than crossed fingers can be a costly mistake.

The Intangible Benefits of the Trade Show

Recognize that sales are not the only objective. Attending a trade show offers a variety of intangible benefits, especially after you've been to one or two. The biggest is the volume of buyers who attend. Where else can you talk in person to a gift-shop owner from Seattle and a gallery owner from Fort Lauderdale at practically the same time? Where else can you meet hundreds of prospective buyers? You reap profits by establishing and maintaining an image not only of a personal nature, but also of goodwill and understanding.

Establishing new relationships is just as important in the long run as filling your production schedule. For example, suppose a buyer has come to the show with a specific budget. He knows what he wants and has completed his shopping for the trip. He comes by your booth and likes what he sees. You develop a business relationship potentially lasting for years. Or suppose this same buyer isn't interested in your wares but knows someone for whose store your line would be perfect and makes the introduction. The what-ifs are endless. Call it being in the right place at the right time. Call it dumb luck. Whatever you call it, the wider your exposure, the greater your chances of expanding.

The trade show also is the perfect setting for acquiring new information and testing new ideas. Bring new products to show along with your regular items. You'll know quickly enough if it generates interest. Trade buyers know their clientele. If a buyer sees something novel and knows he can sell it in his store, he'll likely buy it from you. On the other hand, he might be attracted to it personally but may not be convinced of its marketability. Even the best ideas can bomb, and you want to know about it before you go into production. Have you ever seen a prospective buyer stop by a booth, pick up an item, and say something like, "Oh, I just love this," then put it down and walk off? At a retail fair, that single buyer is representing himself, but at a trade show, he might represent an entire market.

You can discover trends at a trade show. Talk to buyers to find out what their regular clients are interested in. Retailers stay in touch with market trends because it helps them stay in business. You, too, can take advantage of the information. How long the trend will last is anybody's guess, but the trade-show floor is where you'll likely find out that interest is beginning to wane.

Crafts trade shows offer a camaraderie not often found in other industries. A show offers an opportunity to network with others in your field. A good example of the value of networking is checking references of buyers. If a buyer places a $500 order with you, you should make an effort to learn if the buyer is dependable (more on qualifying the buyer later in this chapter).

Do not expect instant monetary success from your first trade show. Trade shows offer more than one opportunity for crafters, and sometimes it takes years to appreciate the dollar value of what at first seems an unlikely contact or a fruitless expedition.

Setting Reasonable Goals

When setting goals and objectives for a show, consider them as tiny facets of a larger goal, say, earning a living from your craft. Begin by writing down what you hope to achieve and express it in a complete sentence. This turns a thought or idea into something tangible. Once on paper, ideas become realities that you must act on, either by following through on them or consciously rejecting them. Start with the largest goal and break it down into smaller segments. The smaller the segments, the more manageable they become. The short-range goals are steps along one or more paths to achieving longer-range ones. Eventually your main goal will be broken down into a large number of small, easily handled tasks, which are goals in themselves. When possible, give each goal a time limit. Then follow the plan methodically, discarding steps that no longer apply and adding others as needed.

Be reasonable about your goals; don't confuse them with desires. You need at least to have a reasonable chance at succeeding and to be realistic about those chances. Setting goals can be a tricky business, especially if success in reaching those goals hinges on factors that are out of your control. For example, you may write, "I will attend the American Craft Council fair in Baltimore next year." You list and follow all of the steps for application. If you're accepted, you then list and follow all of the steps to get to the show. But what if you are not accepted? Once you send in your application, you have no control over the selection process. A more realistic goal, until you are an established exhibitor at one or more shows, is simply to apply to a certain number of shows during a specific time frame, such as "I will apply to six shows over the following year." Your goal to apply is something that is in your complete control.

Realistic sales goals are a slightly different matter, because you cannot predict buyers' actions. But you still have some control over this set of goals. The key word is *realistic*. Say you are planning for your first show and set a goal of writing orders totaling one thousand pieces. This may be unrealistic because, first, you don't know the buyers' minds. Suppose you took orders for only five hundred pieces? Would you think of that as a failure? Second, you can't force people to buy. A more realistic sales goal might read, "I will initiate personal contact with fifty buyers." Not only is this realistic, but it's attainable. Through your research on a particular show, you already know who the buyers are, and you've sent these buyers a preshow promotion to familiarize them with you and your wares. Again, once you're established, it's easier to set figures.

Production goals also are under your control. If you find that for the next six months, you have more work than you can handle by yourself, just list the steps it takes to increase production. It may require streamlining your operation and even hiring employees.

In setting goals, also consider alternative ways of achieving them. Few destinations have only one road leading to them, and few goals have only one course of action necessary for their achievement.

Selecting a Trade Show

The major crafts trade shows across the country and throughout the year range from high-end production and one-of-a-kind crafts shows to gift shows to country- and folk-art shows, all of which attract thousands of buyers. Dozens of smaller, locally produced crafts shows fill market niches of their own. And there are myriad shows that are not exclusive to the crafts world, but nonetheless fertile ground for an enterprising crafter.

Many show promoters send prospectuses to potential exhibitors. Request one and read it. The first and most important factor in selecting a show is the audience. What kind of buyers, and how many of them, does the show attract? The underlying question is in what kinds of shops, stores, or galleries you want your wares to be sold. Buyers come from all over, and it's to your best interest to know where they come from.

One way to find out is to work backward. Spend some time visiting a wide selection of outlets. Ask the owners which shows they attend and why. While you're at it, you can always make your pitch and set up new accounts. (A prerequisite for acceptance to some shows is that you already maintain or have maintained a wholesale account.) Also talk to owners of shops where you would not consider selling your crafts. This information gives you an idea of what shows to stay away from.

Ask other crafters which shows they attend and why. Understand, however, that established crafters tend to stick with shows that are successful for them. Sometimes the reasons for their success are not so easy to pin down, and show loyalty plays an important role.

How Much Does It Cost?

The cost of attending a trade show is more than just the booth fee. When you apply to a show, usually a booth deposit must accompany the application. How much is it and when is the balance due? If you have to cancel, how much of the fee will be refunded? Do you have to pay extra for drapes, tables and chairs, electricity, or an Internet connection, or are these costs included in the booth fee? What about the cost of hiring union labor to unload and set up your booth? Does the promoter pre-pay wages of union laborers? Does the trade show you wish to attend require that you be a dues-paying member of the sponsoring organization? (Don't discount the benefits of membership beyond trade-show participation. Examine the other benefits offered; they might be just what you need.) What about shipping, travel, and accommodations costs?

What does the show promoter provide? Some provide poles and drapes, for example, to separate one booth space from the next. Some spaces merely are marked on the floor. How you design your booth depends on this, as well as the booth size. A high booth fee may seem exorbitant at first, but it may include amenities you otherwise would have to pay for out-of-pocket.

The trade-show environment is geared to bring buyers and sellers together. Show management strives to make the atmosphere as conducive as possible for the success of both ventures. Generally, how you sell is up to you. But often there are some restrictions, and you should know about them in advance. Do you have to show your own work, or may you send a representative? May you serve snacks in your booth? Is there a limit to the number of personnel allowed in your booth at one time? May you share your booth with another crafter or sublease a portion?

The location of the show is probably one of the easiest things to make a decision about, but knowing what city the show will be in isn't enough. Will the show be held in a convention center, sports arena, or hotel? Will it be downtown or in the suburbs? Are hotels within walking distance, or will you have to commute? If you drive to the show in a camper or RV, will you be able to stay overnight in the parking lot, or will you have to drive to an RV park?

Timing is another consideration. Trade-show promotion is a business in its own right. Cities compete with one another by building convention centers to attract large groups of people who will spend money on the local economy. Trade-show promoters take advantage of these large facilities to attract as many crafters and buyers as possible. Lots of crafters mean lots of buyers, lots of buyers mean lots of crafters.

Trade-show promoters also compete for exhibitors and buyers. Some shows are scheduled to coincide, and show promoters often cooperate by providing shuttle service between sites. For you, the exhibiting crafter, this can be good or bad. On the negative side, a competing show can draw buyers away from your booth. On the positive side, the competing show might attract buyers who will visit your show and your booth because it is convenient. Buyers take advantage of the situation merely because they can do more in one trip, provided the buyer is interested in what each show has to offer. The same can be considered true for the crafter. If competing shows run simultaneously, consecutively, or overlap by a day or two, it may be possible—with help and good planning—to exhibit at both.

When to Start

Selecting one or more trade shows at which to exhibit can be arduous and time-consuming. Consider the time spent as an investment in your business. The best time to begin zeroing in on your first trade show is a year and a month before the show you hope to attend. This gives you plenty of time to meet application criteria and show deadlines and to prepare and distribute preshow promotions. Assuming it's an annual event, the extra month is to allow you to arrange to attend the show as a guest before you attend as an exhibitor. True, this is an added expense, but if you discover the show is not for you, you save in the long run. You can see for yourself what kinds of wares are exhibited and who the buyers are. You can ask questions of exhibitors and of show management.

Although trade shows are not open to the public (with the exception of those that offer both trade and retail days), as a crafter you may be able to acquire a guest pass to the show. Call or email the promoter and explain that you wish to visit the show before you apply to exhibit, asking for a guest pass.

If you know a fellow crafter who plans to attend a certain show, ask if you can go along as a booth worker. Being an assistant is an excellent way to learn the ropes before heading out to sea on your own.

Application procedures vary with each promoter, and you'll learn a lot by exploring show websites. Look for the Frequently Asked Questions (FAQ) page, show prospectus, or show manual.

The Jury Process of Selecting Exhibitors

Getting into trade shows and fairs that target unique sets of buyers isn't as easy as submitting an application and paying your booth fee. Show promoters have strict guidelines for choosing exhibitors. Promoters know their market and need to ensure that what they make available during a show is what the buyers expect. Promoters want to know exactly what you plan to exhibit. Your work will be selected on quality, design, originality, function, and countless subjective criteria. In addition, show management wants to know what portion of your work is production, custom, and one of a kind.

The jury process is a long-established method of selecting exhibitors, by which your work is judged on its merit and how it fits into the show's established criteria. Some shows have a seated jury of crafters and other industry professionals who use a point system to select exhibitors. Other promoters use a more relaxed approach, an internal committee perhaps, which considers not only the quality of the work itself, but also the applicant's professional standing in the crafts community. Nevertheless, standards are usually high, and your best chance is to strive to meet them.

If the jury is a time-honored process for selecting exhibitors, the process itself has undergone a massive change as a direct result of digital photography and the Internet. In the past, an applicant submitted by mail a specified number of 35mm images of the work he or she proposed to exhibit, along with a slide of the booth. The images were projected on a large screen for jurors to examine. Today mounted images have given way to digital images, submitted electronically or by mail on a CD. Applications, too, may be submitted electronically.

The Internet has made possible a new service that benefits promoters and applicants. Companies like ZAPP Software and Juried Art Services (see the appendix) handle applications for dozens, if not hundreds, of trade shows and fairs across the country. You can apply for several shows at the same place. Submission fees may apply. Once the show promoter accepts your application, you will receive an invitation to exhibit.

Images you submit must be representative of what you will be exhibiting. If you exhibit something other than what has been selected by a jury, those items may be removed from your booth, or worse, you may forfeit your space.

The importance of submitting high-quality images cannot be overstressed. Photography, not to mention crafts photography, is an art in itself. If you're a capable photographer, shoot the work yourself. The ZAPP website has a selection of examples of good and poor images. Make sure yours are the best, even if you have to hire a studio photographer.

When discussing your needs with a photographer, make sure you explain exactly what you expect from the finished product. If necessary, show him or her similar pictures from trade magazines or drawings of how you want your pieces to appear. The more information you provide, the less the photographer will have to guess your needs. Guesswork often yields unsatisfactory results.

When projected on-screen, many craft items—jewelry, for example—appear much larger than life. Often these shots give no reference to actual size. Suppose you have a delicate porcelain cup that is only two inches tall. Will the juror see it as it really is or mistake it for a large piece of crockery? Make sure your work is photographed in such a way as to prevent ambiguity.

Another good reason for using only images of the best quality is that if your work is selected, the promoter may want to use one of your images for promotional literature. You also can use these shots for your own promotional literature, as well as for advertising in trade journals.

Jurors are people just like you. No matter how objective they try to be, they have their own biases and standards that will cause them to reject some applications. In many cases, a jury won't tell the applicant the reasons for its decision to reject an application. As the rejectee, you are left in the dark. "What did I do wrong?" you ask. You may never know. Perhaps you did nothing wrong at all. It's another instance where luck can play a big role.

Newcomers also should be aware of the seniority system. Those who exhibited last year have a chance to do so again this year. Exhibitors may be assigned seniority points for each successive year they exhibit, which apply to the following year's show. Some shows offer multiyear contracts under which further screenings are not necessary, provided there is no change in products. Some promoters offer sabbaticals to tenured exhibitors. For a small fee, these exhibitors can opt to stay away from a show or shows for a year without losing seniority.

Preshow Promotion

A valuable tool available for the trade-show exhibitor is preshow promotion. This is a mailing sent to buyers who will or might attend the show. Check with the promoter to see if a mailing list is available. If not, compile your own list. Ask the promoter about sources.

Attending trade shows is routine for buyers. They attend whether you do or not. So what's the purpose of a preshow promotion? It's a personal invitation from you not only to attend the show, but also to stop by your booth. If the buyer doesn't know you and is not familiar with your work, the promotion serves as an introduction. With regular customers, the preshow promotion gives you a perfect opportunity to show them what's new in your line. If you have made changes in your line or have new products, don't wait until just before the show to let your regular buyers know about them. Once you've established a mailing list, make it work for you. Your promotion can be a package of information that includes sales literature, price list, and order form, or it can be as simple as a postcard with photographs of your work. For your regular customers, add a personal note. Don't forget to include your booth number.

What Buyers Want

The chief purpose for a buyer attending a show is, of course, to buy. Crafters, buyers, and show promoters have mutually beneficial relationships. Crafters want to show their wares to as large an audience as possible, buyers want handmade crafts to fill their galleries and shops, and promoters want to bring together as many buyers and crafters as possible in an atmosphere conducive to sales. One group's success spells success for all groups. But all have a more basic need: to earn a living.

You go shopping because you have a want or a need. Perhaps it's a pair of shoes you're after. This much you know. When you set off for the shoe store, however, you may not know exactly what kind of shoes you will buy. And, as often happens, you might end up purchasing, along with the shoes, something you had no idea you wanted or needed. The same is true for the crafts buyer.

Crafts buyers know their stores and their clients. They have a general idea of what they can and will sell and what they can't and won't. Sometimes buyers get their shopping done quickly. They have studied catalogs and preshow promotions and know exactly which booths they will visit. But sometimes they have just an idea of what they want and will know for sure only when they see it.

One of the biggest mistakes crafters can make is not identifying their market. To make up for it, they offer a wide and diverse array of goods, hoping to be all things to all buyers. Buyers want a cohesive line of products to choose from, however, not an eclectic mix. They come to the trade show for diversity, to the crafter for specifics. When buyers visit your booth, you don't want to present an overwhelming assortment. Buyers don't want to see a forest; they want to focus on the best one or two trees in it. On the other hand, a booth that is sparsely stocked is not very appealing. Step away from your booth and try to see it as a buyer would.

Once a buyer sees something he's interested in, he automatically registers an expected retail price, then halves it. If your wholesale price is within a reasonable margin of his estimate, you might have a sale. A buyer wants to know as soon as possible what your price points are. If your booth is not busy, he can walk right up and inquire. But if it is busy, what then? He has to wait his turn—just to see if the price is right. Buyers want displays with wholesale prices clearly marked. Also have plenty of preprinted order forms readily available so that the buyer can begin filling one out while waiting to talk with you.

Exclusivity

Buyers often seek exclusivity from their crafts suppliers. Exclusivity guarantees that one buyer is the sole representative of a crafter's work or line of products in a specific geographic area. Exclusivity clauses in sales contracts cover several aspects a crafter should be aware of. Signing a contract for exclusive rights can enhance a buyer-seller relationship, as well as put the crafter on firm footing in a geographic area. Because competition is thus restricted, buyers may be inclined to order more of your work. However, exclusivity also can tie up your work in a certain area and even keep you from competing with the retailer.

An obvious question is, "If I can sell fifty pieces to buyer A with exclusivity, why is that so different from selling ten pieces each to buyers A, B, C, D, and E without exclusivity?" The answer might be "Nothing is different," especially if you will reach a larger and more varied market, and competition is fair and equitable.

Competition, or the control of it, is a key factor in exclusivity arrangements. Few businesses willingly seek out competition, and crafts businesses are no exception. If competition is the servant of the consumer and exclusivity is the friend of the retailer, then who is on the side of the maker? Where exclusivity is concerned, the crafter can rely on a good contract.

Although exclusive rights work in favor of the retailer, they can benefit the crafter as well. But the crafter first must ask, "What's in it for me?" Presumably, the buyer seeking exclusivity will work harder promoting your work. Be sure the terms of promotion are spelled out. You may be able to include in the contract the right of approval of advertising and promotional material, as well as retail price. Because an exclusivity clause puts you under certain restraints, it also can be turned in your favor if it requires the store to purchase a certain volume of merchandise from you.

Carefully consider the period of the agreement and the geographic area in which it is in effect. Keep the period short—no more than a year. You can always renew the contract, but you don't want a time restriction to keep you from growing. You should also think twice about geographic restrictions. In a small town, geographic exclusivity can be fine. But if a contract covers an entire metropolitan area, it can be a disaster. It's better to seek limitations in smaller chunks of the city.

A particular problem when you live in the same area as the exclusive buyer is that you may be prevented from selling retail or wholesale from your shop or studio. The clause also might stipulate that you may sell only a certain number of items or that you must pay a commission on any sales you make to the party holding exclusive rights. Read the contract carefully and make sure you understand all its provisions.

Salesmanship at the Wholesale Level

One of the largest categories in any help-wanted section is sales. Thousands of companies continually seek people with just the right qualifications to hawk everything from automobiles to zippers. Turnover is high in the sales world, because competition is fierce and competent salespeople are few. Some people were born to sell; others seemingly were shortchanged when it came to that nebulous quality known as salesmanship. Indeed, when interviewing people for this book, I met a few exhibitors who said, "You don't want to talk to me. I really don't make any money at this." Yet the enterprising crafter need not be an ace salesperson to accomplish sales goals. But a few aspects of the larger sales world can be of benefit.

Selling crafts at wholesale events, like many other forms of selling, is selling by confrontation. This doesn't mean you accost buyers and nag them into buying. Rather, it means meeting them face-to-face to explain why they should buy what you have to offer. The advantage of trade shows over other kinds of confrontational selling is the number of buyers gathered to confront you, the seller.

Yet just being there is not always enough. You, the maker, have tremendous power to influence a sale. The object is to refine that power to your advantage. A big factor of influence is your firsthand knowledge of your craft and your products. Buyers of American-made crafts, both wholesale and retail, are eager to know something about you and your product. A carefully prepared presentation of what you do and how you do it is invaluable. When you provide this background to the wholesale buyer, she in turn can do the same for her retail customers. In a sense, you are setting the example, or standard, by which future sales of your goods are set. You also have the opportunity here to demonstrate various applications of your crafts that might not be readily apparent. People are always interested in new and different ways to use things.

Engaging the Buyer

At any show or sales event, you have perhaps no more than eight seconds to engage a prospective customer. Eye contact may be your first opening. It's an automatic connection between the two of you signaling the possibility of further communication, and it's your cue to make an invitation to come closer. Another cue is when a browser picks up a brochure or other item from your exhibit. Come prepared with a few open-ended questions, such as "Do you have anything like this in your shop?" or "How do you think your regular customers would respond to this?" Anything that encourages conversation about your crafts and how they will fit into the buyer's world will do. Listen attentively to the answers. Attentive listening—with sincere, other-focused responses—is something everyone appreciates.

Encourage the prospect to handle your product. Have her feel the texture and weight of it. If it's something wearable, have her try it on. If it's a musical instrument, give her a quick lesson. If it's something mechanical, let her see for herself how easy it is to operate. Your product won't sell itself unless you give it every opportunity to do so.

When engaging a prospective buyer, also pay attention to your spatial relationship. *Proxemics* is the branch of human communication that deals with the proximity of persons in a given transaction. Studies in human communication reveal four zones in which communication takes place:
- public (twelve feet and beyond)
- social-consultative (four to twelve feet)
- personal (eighteen inches to four feet)
- intimate (nine to eighteen inches)

The limited size of the trade-show booth automatically puts people, at different stages of a transaction, into one or more of the last three zones. All people claim as their own the intimate space around themselves. As people move closer together, they indicate a willingness to become more involved with one another, even if only on a business level.

When dealing with others, we give hundreds of nonverbal, and usually involuntary, clues about our feelings toward the other person. These clues indicate the propriety of coming closer together, both spatially and emotionally, or the time to stop and even back away. Encroaching too quickly or aggressively into another's intimate zone can be disastrous to a sale. On the other hand, as professional salespersons are well aware, gaining access to another's intimate zone is, in a sense, a victory over that person. Then it's only a matter of when to sign on the dotted line. Anyone who's bought a car from a dealer has experienced this.

Proxemics is another reason to keep booths open and uncluttered. It gives buyers a chance to ease themselves into a situation. A too-close booth tends to thrust the seller and the buyer, or several buyers for that matter, into one another's intimate zone. A counter display is an automatic boundary that enables a quick getaway for an uninterested buyer.

Qualifying the Buyer

Engaging the buyer provides you with some very important information—it indicates a level of seriousness. Professional salespeople call this "qualifying the buyer." Not all attendees have buying as their primary objective. They, too, may be there simply to maintain relationships or observe trends. They may be there just for the fun of it. Some may drop by your booth simply out of curiosity. Maybe your jewelry attracted the attention of a buyer merely for personal reasons. If that buyer owns a gallery that focuses on pottery, your chances of making a significant sale are slim.

Begin qualifying the buyer by asking questions that require other than yes or no answers. Instead of asking, "Do you like this?" ask, "What do you like about this?" Just like any other person, a buyer wants—in fact, needs—acknowledgment. Ask qualifying questions about his business. "How do you think this product would do in your store?" or "How do you think your regular customers would receive this?" Of course, it doesn't hurt to ask questions that are more specific about the buyer's length of time in business, the nature of the shop or gallery, and the clientele. Eventually you will want this information anyway, if an order is placed. Whatever questions you ask, listen attentively to the answers and give good feedback, verbal and nonverbal, indicating that you've heard and understood the message. Attentive listening is a bridge builder.

You can judge by the answers how much interest the buyer has in your product and whether he is considering placing an order. A lot of times, it's nothing more than a hunch. If you determine that the buyer is not interested and is trying to get away, bow out of the conversation gracefully. The uninterested buyer may know someone looking for exactly what you have to sell, so it doesn't pay to be even subtly rude. Word-of-mouth advertising is a mainstay in the crafts business.

Each time you talk to a buyer, request a business card. On the back of the card, note the buyer's qualifications as a potential customer. Rate buyers on an interest scale from, say, zero to five, where zero indicates no interest, five the greatest interest. Also indicate whether the buyer's outlet is appropriate for your crafts. An efficient and orderly alternative is to bring with you a lead form that you can fill out as you talk with the prospect or as soon as possible after the visit. Your form should include a space for the prospect's name and contact information, business name, market, and rating that indicates level of interest. Include a place to take notes about the nature of the conversation and even a personal description of the prospect so that when you get home you can more easily associate the person with the information. After talking to dozens of people, names and faces become a blur. Staple the business card to the form to keep them together. This information will be useful later, when you follow up after the show (see chapter 9).

Of course, if you take an order on the spot, you'll need to collect more details; those points are discussed later in this chapter under "Checking References."

Ask for the Order

The most important question you can ask, the toughest qualifier of them all, is "Can I take your order?" Simply asking the question may sway a hesitant buyer in your direction.

While working on a sale, it often is necessary to demonstrate why your product is better than that of a competitor. After all, part of your job is to convince the buyer why she should buy from you instead of someone else. There is nothing wrong with this, provided it is done honestly and with respect for the competitor. Avoid disparaging your competitor or her products. It's unprofessional and unethical, and it indicates a negative attitude, which the buyer may perceive to be a pervasive quality of your business. Besides, it's a small world, and chances are good that criticism will come back to you.

Another negative to avoid is apologizing for your prices. If you must apologize, then your prices are wrong. And it doesn't pay to explain how difficult it is to make a living as a crafter. Most buyers already know this, especially those who are in business for themselves.

A buyer who expresses even a little interest although she does not place an order at the show is a qualified prospect. You already have contact information, and this is a good lead to follow up on after the show.

Positions, Please

Your booth includes a chair or two, intended for the comfort of buyers. There is no law, written or unwritten, that says you can't or shouldn't sit in a chair while tending your booth. But there is a psychological advantage to standing. It makes you look eager and interested. Imagine a scene where a buyer approaches a booth and the crafter is seated, perhaps reading a book. The crafter looks up and asks, "May I help you?"

"Of course you can help me," the buyer thinks. "That's what you're here for, isn't it?"

So much for first impressions.

Body posture and orientation also play important roles in communication. In most transactional situations, the more relaxed party is usually the one with the higher status. But a too-relaxed posture can indicate boredom and lack of interest. Bodily orientation refers to the position of the shoulders of the two people within the transaction. The best communication occurs when two people have their shoulders squared with one another and they are face-to-face, also called vis-à-vis. As the shoulders begin to open out into a V, channels of communication begin to close. The more people deviate from the face-to-face posture, the less positive the communication. Transitions in communication are usually accompanied by shifts in posture and orientation, no matter how subtle.

After you and the buyer have become acquainted and it appears a sale is imminent, it may be appropriate for both of you to sit. (If possible, however, avoid sitting if the buyer can't sit as well.) This major shift in posture and orientation indicates an obvious, not to mention positive, shift in the transaction. People are content to stand while listening to others, but they usually are more comfortable seated while reading, writing, or closing a deal.

Personal contact is the most important aspect of salesmanship, regardless of the skill level. When buyer and seller know one another and have developed a level of trust for one another, current and future business dealings are enhanced.

Taking the Edge Off

Working at fairs and shows can be grueling, both physically and emotionally. If possible, take along an assistant to help tend the booth. It is imperative, however, that an assistant be as professional and well versed in your craft and your product as you are. Your assistant should be able to demonstrate the product, answer any questions, make sales, and take orders. An assistant who merely says to a prospective client, "I'm only the helper; the owner is taking a break but should be back in twenty minutes," is no helper at all. You may be back in twenty minutes, but will the buyer? To get the most out of each day, you have to be alert at all times. You do not want to appear haggard or ill at ease. Frequent breaks, one every two or three hours, are often necessary to help maintain composure and comportment.

Sales Aids

Many wholesale crafts buyers are interested in the background of the products and the crafters who produce them. One of the best sales aids you can employ is the hangtag, attached to or packaged with each item. Hangtags describe the item, noting any special features, uses, or processes of manufacture. They also might include a few pertinent words about the maker. Hangtags are valuable sales aids for you because they are valuable sales aids for the buyer, who ultimately will sell your wares to the public. Anything you can tell the buyer about your craft can be useful in selling the craft at the retail level.

All trade shows, regardless of the industry, are stomping grounds for literature gatherers. You can recognize them by their heavy giveaway plastic tote bags, one in each hand. They visit each booth and collect as much literature as they can. Where this literature ends up is anyone's guess. Although most trade-show promoters are vigilant in qualifying buyers before they enter the building, some literature gatherers do get by. This is especially true at shows that feature retail days open to the public. Be sure to bring enough brochures to satisfy some voracious literary appetites.

Price lists and order forms should be clear and easy to follow. Keeping these two items readily available enables buyers to begin writing their own orders if you are busy.

Another valuable sales aid is a step-by-step pictorial or actual exhibit of how your craft item is produced. This should be no more complicated than is necessary. Rely on visual elements rather than written descriptions. Take, for example, a woman who makes elegant cast-metal figurines. A simple revolving case holds a piece representing each step of the process, beginning with the wax original and ending with the final product.

When it comes to sales literature, be brief. In the busy trade-show environment, few people care to spend their time reading. They prefer to see and hear.

Two more sales aids that may be useful are volume discounts and display cases, but be sure your price structure can handle it. Though volume discounts may boost sales, they may not pay off in dollars. Whether or not you offer volume discounts, always establish a minimum order. Some crafters provide buyers with a display case or rack when it's appropriate for a particular product. You can sell these outright or offer them free of charge for an initial order of a specific size.

Finally, there's your business card. Make it attractive, as befits a crafter. Having said that, however, note that technology is rendering even the time-honored business card obsolete. With the increasing use of smartphones and tablets, business cards are going the way of the money clip and checkbook. Apps like Bump (see the appendix) make exchanging contact information, including your photo, as fast and easy as a knuckle bump.

Checking References

Buying and selling transactions conducted at a trade show—where orders are written instead of goods exchanged on the spot—are based on mutual trust. The crafter trusts that the buyer will pay promptly when billed; the buyer trusts that the merchandise will be delivered as promised. It's a delicate but necessary balance between two professionals.

Until a firm relationship between the two businesses is established, a specter of doubt lurks that one party or the other may not follow through. Consider the gallery owner with cash-flow problems who deems your bill a low priority. Or consider the crafter who is overbooked and months behind schedule and can't deliver on time. In either case, the person's reputation is at stake. News travels fast in both communities.

So what can the crafter do to help ensure that the buyer is reliable? Some things you may want to know include the following:
- buyer's name, business name, address, and phone number
- business owner's name and length of time in business
- references in the form of crafters with whom the buyer has done business, preferably any who are attending the show

- authorization to check financial references
- bank and account information

For the purposes of market research, also obtain a brief profile of the business, asking for the following information:

- typical clientele, including whether it consists of tourists, walk-ins, or regulars, as well as the age group
- general description of inventory, including the type of craft, such as pottery, woodwork, or jewelry, as well as whether it is high-end or low-end
- setting and atmosphere of store, including whether it is a storefront or in a mall, and in a high- or low-traffic area

Some buyers may bring with them copies of their references with further information about their businesses; similarly, you can provide new buyers with a list of clients with whom you've done business. Retail outlets with good credit are willing to give references because they are eager to do business with you. Just the same, a presentation of references should not be construed as proof of reliability. It is not necessary to check references before completing an order, but you should do so as soon as possible after the show. Checking references may seem unnecessary, especially after a friendly conversation, but it can eliminate problems in the long run.

Terms

For new accounts, some sellers insist on cash on delivery (COD) or some percentage of the sale price as a down payment before delivery of the first order. Although this appears to be a good move on the crafter's part, many buyers consider this a nuisance and an inconvenience. Not only does it interrupt cash flow for the buyer, but it indicates a level of distrust as well. And what recourse does the shop owner have if the merchandise is already paid for but arrives in broken or otherwise unsalable condition? Regardless of what buyers think about the practice, however, it makes sense to discuss COD terms with new accounts if you have any doubts about reliability.

The most common billing terms are "net 30," which means that the entire payment is due within thirty days of delivery, provided that the shipment is accompanied by an invoice, or otherwise within thirty days of receipt of the invoice. A variation of this is "2/10/30," which is intended as an incentive for quick payment. This allows the buyer to deduct 2 percent of the total bill if it is paid within ten days. Two percent may not seem like much, especially on a small order, but if the buyer has been offered enough of these discounts from various accounts, it could add up to a substantial sum. On the other hand, the buyer may elect not to take advantage of the discount. It's a small price to pay for the use of your money for twenty or more days.

When the order is placed, the buyer and seller agree on the terms and shipping arrangements, including who pays for shipping and the approximate date or dates of delivery. If you will be including a handling fee or other charges, now is the time to mention this. Buyers don't appreciate hidden or added charges, especially when they discover them on the bill. They make their decision to buy based on your wholesale price. If you subsequently jack up the total cost with additional charges, they are not getting the deal they bargained for. They will feel they may have been better off going to a competitor who includes all extra costs in the wholesale price.

Miscellany

So far, this chapter has outlined the basics of selling crafts at wholesale events. Many other minor aspects of the business require less discussion but are important as well. This section serves as a catchall, a tying of loose ends.

Unions

All major trade shows across the nation are held in union facilities. Unions are stronger in some cities than in others. Depending on how large your exhibit is, you may have to deal in some way with one or more unions. Which ones will depend on the city, the relative strength of the local unions, and what they will allow you to get away with. Check with the show promoter in advance for union policies.

Whether your exhibit arrives by motor carrier (truck) or you bring it with you, laborers from the Teamsters union usually will claim the right to unload and cart your exhibit to your booth. A possible exception is if your exhibit is small, with few elements that you can carry by hand one or two at a time. Don't, however, bother looking for a hand truck or dolly to make things easier, because you will find a union worker at the controls.

Carpenters have jurisdiction over uncrating and assembling, as well as disassembling and re-crating, your exhibit and may claim the right to do so. Other tasks within the purview of carpenters are laying carpet, draping tables, hanging signs, and other decorating chores. If your exhibit has an electrical component, an electrician also may be involved in the setup.

Flameproofing

Exhibitors are responsible for ensuring that their exhibits are fire-resistant. Be prepared for the fire marshal to turn up at your booth before the show opens. Merchandise is excluded from this regulation, but fabric draping and other easily combustible material may have to be certified as flameproof. Fire-retardant products are available from major hardware outlets. You may have to hire a locally certified company to do the flameproofing for you on-site. Check with show management for more information about meeting this requirement.

Selling Samples

The products you bring to the trade show are samples of what you will ultimately produce for the buyer. Unless you are attending a combined wholesale-retail show, you need bring only enough samples (along with replacements in case of damage) to adequately represent your line. Some show promoters allow you to sell these samples, usually at the end of the show. Other promoters may disallow the practice. Check with show management for policies.

Dealing with Large Orders

At the typical trade show, several buyers place orders with a given crafter. With luck, the income from these combined orders will last you a long while and there will be enough diversity in buyers as a hedge against cancellation of some orders and slow payment on others. But consider the hypothetical story of the fiber artist who received a single order so large that the only way she could meet the demand was to dramatically increase her production capabilities. Based on the strength of the order, she negotiated a bank loan to add on to her studio and purchase a large quantity of materials. Midway through construction, the buyer canceled the order.

Though not common, such a catastrophe can happen. To guard against a situation like this, ask for half the money as a down payment. If the buyer hesitates, consider an escrow account. This is an account with a third party, usually a bank. Money held in escrow cannot be released to you until the merchandise is delivered, and it will be returned to the buyer by a specified date should you be unable to fulfill the order. For both parties, it serves as an incentive and a guarantee.

Delivery of big orders also can be spread out over time according to a predetermined schedule. This keeps you from having to store a large amount of merchandise awaiting a single shipment. It requires more paperwork and possibly higher shipping charges, but it also may help the buyer's cash flow—and yours.

Coping with Stress

Who among us is not familiar with stress and its effects on body and mind? The trade-show environment comes with a host of stress-causing situations, of which many cannot be avoided, and some can only be eased.

One of the biggest stressors, especially for first-time exhibitors, is concern over monetary success at the show. You can do only so much to swing success in your direction. Nevertheless, the more immediate your need of financial gain, the greater the opportunity for stress and anxiety to creep in. Remember, financial reward is not the only form success takes at a trade show. Go to the show with the intention of making new contacts and establishing new relationships, gaining experience and exposure, and increasing your knowledge and understanding of the system. All these have the potential for stimulating future sales.

Preshow stress can be handled most effectively by research, planning, and preparation. Just knowing what's in store does much to alleviate stress. Procrastination often plays a part in adding to stress. But procrastination is a symptom of stress, not a cause of it. Stave off procrastination by making a schedule and sticking to it. Break large goals into smaller ones, and tick them off one at a time and over plenty of time. Small successes accumulate into large ones. Success is wonderful therapy for stress and procrastination.

Success is not a cure-all for stress, however. Indeed, success can also *cause* stress. One danger lies in taking more orders than you possibly can fulfill in the foreseeable future. Your alternatives are attempting to renegotiate shipping schedules later on or beefing up your operation with more equipment and employees, both of which may cause their own forms of stress. Be honest with buyers about your production schedule. What's more, you can always stop taking orders if necessary.

Coping with the rigors of the trade-show floor also can be tough. The din, the press of bodies, the constant pitching, the hours of standing on a concrete floor—all take their toll. Cut back on the damage by taking enough breaks to remain sharp and alert. Only you know how much stress you can withstand before it affects your performance. Dress comfortably. The crafts trade does not have a rigid dress code. Comfortable shoes that provide adequate support are especially important, because you'll be standing most of the day. But don't buy a new pair of shoes right before the show; give yourself some time to break them in or you may be in for a few days of torture.

A powerful stressor comes from above, if you exhibit in a hall lighted by halogen lights. Not only does halogen lighting, with its greenish cast, play havoc on the colors in your exhibit, but it also can cause headaches, blurred vision, and fatigue. Take frequent breaks to avoid overexposure.

If you're thinking that dressing comfortably and taking plenty of breaks seems an overly simplistic approach to dealing with stressors, you're right. Adequately coping with stress involves three senses not associated with the basic five senses of touch, smell, taste, sight, and hearing. They are the sense of commitment, the sense of control, and the sense of challenge.

Being committed to family, work, a cause, or just about anything helps overcome a sense of alienation. Performance suffers when we feel uninvolved. We do things merely because they must be done, not because we enjoy doing them.

All of us need to feel in control of our lives and our destinies. A lack of control makes us feel like victims of circumstances, without influence over events affecting us. Making things happen instead of letting things happen greatly reduces stress.

A sense of challenge means an ability to deal with change. Things not within our control often force us to make changes. The challenge comes after we recognize we don't have control over certain situations. Instead of feeling victimized, search for ways to learn and grow from the situation. If you lack a sense of challenge, then change is a threat rather than a catalyst.

These aspects of stress management apply to every aspect of life. But since the crafts trade show is relatively simple compared with many other facets of life, it is easy to apply the principles of commitment, control, and challenge to that arena.

After the Show

The end of the final day of the show has come. The doors close for the last time on the buyers who time and again made their way up and down the aisles. You leave the arena a changed person, wiser for the experience. You've gained new insights into the industry, met new people, and obtained new ideas for improving your business.

Evaluating the Show

Ideally, you will leave the trade show with pockets stuffed full of orders. But do you know how well you really did? Was it even worthwhile? Spend some time as soon after the show as possible to evaluate the results. Go back to your list of objectives and reexamine them. How many promising contacts did you make? Did you learn anything new about the crafts business in general and your business in particular? Did you get any ideas for new products or learn about a new trend?

And did you meet your sales goal? Tally your orders and check them against your production schedule. Will you cover your costs? Will you make a profit? Will you have to do another show sooner than you had expected or take other measures to sell more products? Will you have to adjust your prices to reflect a truer picture of trade-show costs or to bring them more in line with the market? If your orders fell short of your goal, remember that not all trade-show business is generated during the show. Many buyers place orders after the show.

Following Up

The show is over. You've gone home, walked through the door, and collapsed on the couch. But to maximize what you've accomplished, there is still one more thing to do: follow up. This is where all those notes you took on the trade-show floor will pay off.

There are two areas in which following up is imperative. The first is with clients who placed orders. The second is with prospective clients who didn't. In the hectic atmosphere of the trade show, mistakes can happen. Mistakes breed misunderstanding. Clearing up misunderstandings long after the fact sometimes takes more effort than making sure they don't exist in the first place. What's more, a valuable business relationship is at risk. The best preemptive strike against misunderstanding is confirmation. Within two weeks of the show, send each buyer—by US mail or email—a thank-you note and a confirmation of the order as you understand it, including product, quantity, price, terms, delivery dates, and shipping costs and arrangements. Personalize your communication with a detail or two about your conversation. This not only helps the buyer place you in context, but also shows a level of goodwill and interest on your part. Ask the buyer to correct any misunderstandings at once or accept the order as it stands.

Don't hesitate to follow up quickly with all the other qualified prospects you encountered and thank them for stopping by your booth. Make good use of your notes to personalize your conversation. Give a brief description of the work and its qualities as a reminder of what you do. Close by suggesting that now that the show is over, perhaps the buyer would like to consider placing an order. Include with the letter or email a brochure, price list, and order form.

chapter 5

Advertising and Publicity: Marketing through Traditional Media

No business can operate within a vacuum. If people don't know what you have to offer, there is no reason for them to come knocking at your door—or your booth. It's through marketing that people know who you are and what you have to offer.

Marketing is a broad practice that includes research, promotion, publicity, and advertising. To be most effective, marketing should be an ongoing, constant reminder that you are in business.

Advertising is the activity of creating and placing specific advertisements in various media. The psychological power of advertising is enormous. A onetime, small, ill-conceived ad suggests that the advertiser is operating on a shoestring (which may be true). This detracts from the apparent value of the product—that is, the value you subjectively apply to your product. Large, snappy ads, especially those that appear regularly, suggest the advertiser is serious about his business and can afford to do things right. It also gives the product or service greater apparent value.

Publicity is attention given to a person, product, or business because of advertising and other forms of promotion. Advertising and publicity go hand in hand, but there is a difference. Advertising is paid for. Any medium will happily exchange its space for your dollars. Publicity is free or costs little, unless you enlist the services of a public relations firm. Once you've paid the price, advertising is automatic. Getting publicity, especially in the media, is not guaranteed. Because it is essentially free advertising, it is the decision of the media whether to grant you access. This decision is based on what it can do for them, not what it can do for you, though the media is well aware of how you benefit.

What Editors Want:
Who, What, When, Where, Why, and How

The basic factors in advertising and publicity, the five Ws and an H, are *who, what, when, where, why*, and *how*. These are essential, though the *why* and the *how* are often implicit rather than explicit. No ad should be without them, except, perhaps, when a product or service is so well known that one factor implies the others.

When two people meet for the first time, the first bit of information that passes between them is who they are; names are exchanged. As an advertiser, this is the first bit of information you want to convey. Buyers, whether retail or wholesale, want to know whom they are dealing with. In many retail transactions, however, the *who* is often overlooked. People see what they like and buy it. The further removed you are from your product, the further removed you are from the buyer. It is up to you to make yourself known. Advertising is how you establish name or product familiarity. In today's multimedia world, it's called *branding*.

The *what* factor is the essence of the message you wish to convey. Perhaps it is your handmade paper. But it could be more general, such as an exclusive showing of your work at a local gallery. In any case, it is the cornerstone of your ad or publicity campaign. The best conveyance of *what* is the illustration; ads are best when they are visual. Even on radio, the best ads are those that paint mental pictures, taking advantage of the power of imagery to get the message across.

If you are celebrating the grand opening of your gallery, the *when* tells the date and time. If your craft is the focus, it tells availability—hours of business, for example. The same holds for the trade show. *Where* takes its cue from *what* and *when*.

Why is often the most difficult message to convey, but it is the most important. It deals more with the psychological and emotional sides of advertising. *Why* deals with the target market's wants and needs. If the main message of the ad is "Celebrate the Grand Opening of Eye of the Beholder Gallery," for example, you also must somehow explain why anyone would want to attend: "Come see the latest in American crafts designed to meet your decorative needs." If you can solve a problem by filling a need, you have a sale. It may be a cliché, but there is a good reason why advertisers talk about "that special gift for that special someone."

How can be aptly described as the "call to action": "Call for a free catalog." Or it can mean inviting buyers to travel one thousand miles to the trade show where you will be exhibiting: "Please drop by and see me at Booth 392 at the Boston Buyers Market."

The Media Release: Free Publicity

The media release provides the public with news, information, and entertainment. As formidable as it sounds, the media release is nothing more than a short piece that informs the media—print, broadcast, or online—that a newsworthy event is about to take place. What is newsworthy is always up to the discretion of the editor who will eventually publish (or ignore) your release. It is imperative, therefore, that your release be pegged to an event.

What is newsworthy? That depends. If you live in a small town in South Dakota and you are going to a trade show in Boston, the editor of the local paper might consider a media release about your trip. Don't bother sending one to the Boston media. But if you are the designer of something new, different, and trendsetting on a national scale—and your idea ties in with, say, an upcoming holiday or event—someone in Boston might be interested. Have evidence to back up your claims. What's interesting news to the editor of a small-town weekly may be an annoyance to an editor at a big-city daily paper.

Your news release must look professional. If you will be sending a hardcopy via mail, write it on your business letterhead. If you're sending it in the body of an email, place less emphasis on format, but apply the same recommendations to content. Avoid sending a release as an attachment if this is your first contact with an editor. It may not be opened.

The copy, the term for the text to be set in type for printing or to broadcast, should be typed double-spaced for easy editing. At the top, type, "For Immediate Release," so that there is no question of intent. Then type, "Contact:" followed by your name and telephone number. Next comes your headline, which must state your message concisely as well as attract the attention of an editor. Editors want to know what you can do for them, and that starts with the headline. And what can you do for an editor? Give him something that will entertain, educate, or solve a problem for his readers.

Then write the lead, which expands on the idea presented in the headline. All five Ws and the H should be as close to the top of the lead as possible, though not necessarily in the first sentence. Determine which of the six elements is most important and begin with that. Follow the lead with less important but relevant background material and a quote or two. Stick to the facts. Don't add self-aggrandizing adjectives or statements. The editor is not interested in your ego, only your news.

Keep it short. If the editor wants more details, you'll get a call or email.

The *media kit* is an extension of the media release providing more information. It consists of a folder that includes brochures, photographs, a business card, a media release, and background information. It also may include copies of other stories published about you and your work.

Whether you send a full media kit or a single-page release, be aware of deadlines. Daily newspapers have the shortest lead time. The deadline for a weekly is usually a week or two before the edition in which you want your story or ad to appear. For magazines, plan on a lead time of three to six months. In any event, check in advance with a phone call. It's also wise to send your material to the right editor, which you can also ask about when you telephone.

Do not be surprised if an editor rewrites your carefully worded media release from beginning to end and even leaves out material. This might happen for several reasons, especially if the paper in which it appears is larger than a small-town weekly. First, in your enthusiasm, you may have missed your own point. It happens all the time. What you think is the most salient point may not really be so; editors are trained to recognize such things. Second, the editor or writer will force your copy to conform to the paper's style. Third, editors know that media releases go to many different places. They don't want their stories to appear word for word in other papers.

Your main concerns with media releases are accuracy and clarity. A fuzzy release produces fuzzy results. If the editor or writer can't follow it, neither can readers.

Sometimes a media release sparks an editor's or reporter's interest. If that happens, you may find yourself the topic of a feature story, complete with interview and photography session. This kind of publicity is invaluable. Frame the article and display it in your booth. Ask the photographer if she will give or sell you additional images for your publicity material.

Learning where to send your media releases and kits is an important part of the marketing process. The shotgun approach is not necessarily the best one. Sending media kits through the US mail to the wrong markets is an unnecessary waste.

Yet it's also time-consuming to search out the thousands of media outlets available. For a relatively small price, you can create custom media lists through Easy Media List. Another alternative is to use a media release distribution service, such as PRWeb. (See the appendix for websites of these and other media services.)

Finally, you can subscribe to Help a Reporter Out (HARO; see appendix). HARO is a subscription service for reporters and potential sources (you). Reporter members put out requests for experts and other sources of information about stories they're working on. These requests come straight to your inbox. HARO offers free and paid subscriptions.

News Stories by Freelance Writers or Staff Reporters: More Free Publicity

A story in a local paper can lead to bigger and better publicity. Consider it gravy if it happens to you. Freelance writers always are on the prowl for good stories. One place they look is in the newspaper. Crafts fairs also are good stomping grounds for specialty writers.

With a freelance writer or staff-written news feature, however, you have even less control over the content of the story than you do with a release-generated story. The freelance writer or staff reporter will write the article his way to suit his own needs. He is well aware of the publicity value of the story, but his interest lies in what you can do for him, not the other way around.

If you have something of regional or national interest, you are a likely candidate for a magazine feature. But you don't have to wait around holding your breath for a freelancer or reporter to get the message. Most areas have local writers' groups. With a little research and networking, you can find out who might be interested in doing a story on you. A media kit, news release, or phone call may net you space in a national publication. Whether your story is published, however, is up to the magazine editor's discretion.

Do you have writing skills? If so, use them to your advantage. The most successful crafters are those with a reputation. Naturally, you are an authority on your craft. Boost your reputation by writing about what you know, which is your business. If you have something worthwhile to share with others in your field and can convey that message clearly, magazine editors are eager to hear from you.

In the end, it is all publicity. And publicity gives you name familiarity. People are more apt buy from people they know than from people they don't.

Promotional Materials and the Media Kit

The media kit is a collection of promotional materials you send to various media outlets to give them more background on you and your company. You can send your media kit through the mail or via email. And you also can display all the information on a media page on your website (see chapter 6).

The media kit might include the following:

- cover letter (optional)
- media release
- good-quality photographs of you and your work, or jpegs if using email
- business card
- résumé or biographical information pertinent to your work
- list of events you regularly attend

Any files you send to the media electronically should include links to your website and other appropriate places on the Internet. Also give your website and email address on any printed material. It's easy to include a quick response (QR) code on business cards, brochures, and other promotional material. A QR code scanned with a smartphone or tablet can take the user directly to your website. You can also create a QR code that has your contact information in it. Many websites offer free code generators (see the appendix). Download the generated jpeg file and paste it into your documents. Paid services offer tracking and other data for QR codes you create.

Fast computers and sophisticated software make it easier than ever to produce your own marketing and promotional materials. But mastering software, designing brochures, and

writing media releases and other promotional pieces is time-consuming. And even the most gifted crafter may not have the necessary writing and graphic skills to put together an effective media package. If that's the case, getting help from one or more professionals may be necessary.

In any case, all your promotional materials should look professional. Written material must be free of grammatical and typographical errors. Graphics should be sharp and clear and arranged in an appealing manner on the page. Taking the time—or spending the money—to do it right will pay off.

chapter 6

Going Global: Marketing and Selling on the Internet

The Internet is the easiest and fastest way to get information. You've probably used it to find suppliers, compare prices, and order products, among other things. Perhaps you used it to find and purchase this book. Even if you don't intend to sell your crafts around the world, your Internet presence will increase your visibility—and your market—in ways the old-fashioned paper Yellow Pages never could. In fact, your business may suffer if it's not easily findable online.

For all its value, however, some people avoid using the Internet as a marketing tool, giving the excuses that it's too expensive, technical, confusing, or time-consuming, or saying that they prefer word-of-mouth marketing. All of these may be true to some extent, but unless you have more business than you can handle, none should prevent you from diving in. But before you do, you'll need to make some decisions. Although how to create a website is beyond the scope of this book, this chapter includes some basic information to get you started.

Your Website: Static or Dynamic?

There are two kinds of websites: static and dynamic. A static site merely displays information and is not interactive. Think of it as an online brochure with unlimited pages. It is composed entirely of pages written in HTML, the most basic language for webpages and the easiest to learn.

A dynamic site allows for interaction among users. A blog is a dynamic site. A site with a shopping cart also is dynamic. A dynamic site takes more time to develop and maintain and will require more technical expertise (yours or someone else's). Dynamic sites are built using a more sophisticated language (PHP, for example) and interact with a separate database. The database contains the information displayed on the page.

Your Domain, Registry, and Hosting Service

To take the best advantage of the Internet, you should have your own domain name. A domain name defines for the owner certain administrative authority on the Internet. What we think of as a domain name, for example, mybusiness.com, is actually a sub-domain of a top-level domain (TLD), such as .com, .net, or .org.

A domain costs about $10 per year, depending on where you buy it (more on that later). Consider your domain name carefully. After you've gone through all the work of establishing your website, you won't want to make changes. An ill-conceived name could be costly.

The best domain name is one that describes your business, but it may not be as easy as that. Millions of domains are registered every year. The name you like may already have been taken. Fortunately, several domain-name search tools are available (see the appendix for a few of them). Here are some tips for choosing a good domain name:

- Keep it short and simple to remember
- Keep it easy to say and to type
- Avoid ambiguous spellings
- Use the .com suffix if possible (it means business, as in commerce)
- Avoid using hyphens to separate words; people are now accustomed to reading words strung together

You initially purchase your domain name from a *registrar* or *registry*. After sixty days, you can transfer the domain to another registrar if you desire. You can register or renew a domain for one or multiple years. When you register a domain in your name, all of your contact information becomes public and is easily searchable through sites like whois.net. You can keep your ownership and contact information hidden by purchasing an add-on service for a small fee, about $3 per year. This will help reduce spam and scam solicitations.

The Internet Corporation for Assigned Names and Numbers (ICANN) administers the domain name system (DNS). For a complete list of registrars, visit the website listed in the appendix. There you will find hundreds of registrars to choose from. Most of them are resellers of domains managed by larger suppliers. Individual registrars vary greatly in what they charge and how they manage your account. To find a registrar, search on "compare domain registrars." When deciding on a registrar, be sure it is ICANN accredited, and run a search for several of your top picks along with the word "review" in the search string in order to read others' reviews of the registrars.

An important function of the registrar is to host your site's domain name server (also DNS). This ensures that when someone types in your site's uniform resource locator, or URL, his or her browser goes to the server where your site's files are. This location is called the *hosting service* or *Web host*.

With thousands of hosting services to choose from, it's hard to know which one is right for you. As when choosing a registrar, run a search for "hosting services" along with the word "review" or "compare." Consider the following criteria in a hosting service:

- price
- uptime
- bandwidth
- customer support

A hosting service for a single domain can range from as $4 to $10 per month, and even less if you enter into a multiyear agreement. These basic accounts are on shared servers, which means you are sharing space and bandwidth with dozens or hundreds of other domains. A more expensive alternative is the dedicated server, which hosts only one domain. Prices for a dedicated server will start around $100 per month. A shared account is sufficient for a small business that has relatively little traffic.

Bandwidth refers to the amount of data transferred to and from a website. It's only a consideration if you have an extraordinary amount of traffic, or if you post lots of video files. Minimal bandwidth allotments will be sufficient for the small crafts business, but it's not unusual today for small accounts to have unlimited bandwidth on shared servers.

Most hosting services advertise their *uptime*, the amount of time their servers are available on the Internet. Ninety-nine percent uptime is typical. The lower you go below this, the more likely you'll lose visitors.

Customer service will be important if you have any questions about setting things up or you encounter any problems with your site along the way. Problems do happen and you'll want them resolved as quickly as possible. The best service is where you can get someone on the phone. Online chat also is good because of its immediacy. With many of the bargain services, the only way to reach customer service is through submitting a support ticket explaining the problem. Then you wait for someone to respond by email.

Although there are many things to consider, too many to list here, a word about security is in order. Keeping servers and websites secure from hackers is an ongoing concern. Not all hosting services are equal in this regard. It is wise to search for reviews of any service you're considering.

You can keep things simple by having your site hosted with your registrar, but it's not necessary. The two can be independent of one another. The only link is through the domain name server, which is specific to the host but set at the registrar; the host gives you the DNS, and you enter the information in your registry.

Registering a domain and purchasing server space are not the only way to have your own website. You can create a free website at wordpress.com, which uses the popular WordPress software. Although this was initially a blogging platform, it's becoming versatile enough to serve as a general website platform. Paid upgrades add some functionality. Here your domain is a subdomain of a larger domain; for example, if your website is called mycraftsbusiness.wordpress.com, wordpress.com is the larger domain, and mycraftsbusiness is the subdomain. In this situation, you do not need to register a domain name.

Don't confuse wordpress.com with wordpress.*org*. From the latter, you can download the WordPress software and install it on your own server; this will give you a self-hosted blog. Used this way, WordPress is highly extensible and customizable, with thousands of plug-ins and themes to choose from.

If you *do* have your own domain and hosting service, many choices are open to you. One of the most widely used site management interfaces is cPanel, which is included with your hosting package. Through your cPanel or other interface, you can create email addresses, view site statistics, manage your site files and databases, and perform several other tasks. It also allows you to install dozens of applications, including WordPress and other site-building software, as well as shopping carts.

Creating and maintaining a website is time-consuming and can be challenging even to the technically inclined. There is a steep learning curve, especially with self-hosted blogs and content management systems (CMS) such as Drupal and Joomla. You may need to hire someone to build your site for you. Websites can be simple or complex. How long it will take to build and how much it will cost depend on a variety of factors. Get several quotes and samples before choosing a website developer you can work with.

eCommerce:
Taking Orders and Payments Online

Selling your crafts from you website adds one or more layers of complexity. If you already have a merchant account, you can install one of several shopping cart packages on your site.

PayPal is one of the most popular payment systems on the Web. A basic account is free, and you do not need a merchant account. Individuals can have one personal account and one business account. With the basic Website Payments Standard account, you can set up a simple shopping cart with buttons you create on the PayPal site. The PayPal button maker creates HTML code that you copy and paste on your website. When a buyer clicks on a button, she is transferred to a page at PayPal linked to your account. The buyer can pay with a credit card or with funds in her own PayPal account if available. You pay a transaction fee of 2.9 percent plus 30 cents. You can create shipping labels for each order directly from the transaction page.

Website Payment Pro offers the same benefits as having a merchant account and payment gateway by combining these services into one package for $30 a month. A major difference between the standard and pro versions is that instead of being transferred to the PayPal site, buyers stay on your site, just as they would with a typical merchant account with a shopping cart setup.

Two final notes about websites. First, putting photographs of your work on the Internet is both a necessity and a curse. It's necessary because the Internet is a place of discovery, the biggest showcase in the world. It may be the first place people look for you or what you have to offer. But it's also a curse because "shoplifting" is so easy. Your great ideas and original designs may show up somewhere else for a fraction of the cost, stolen by unscrupulous individuals who are delighted to make money off you. *All* crafters take this risk when they promote themselves on the Internet.

Second, avoid putting your home address and phone number on your website. Unless you have a separate storefront or studio, use a post office box. Have a dedicated business phone line or mobile number where customers can reach you—but not other members of your family. Privacy is an increasing concern in this age of easy global communication. Even though you want to be found easily as a crafter, you also need to create a barrier, however small, between your family and the rest of the world.

Selling from Online eCommerce Sites

One of the marvels of the Internet is that you can sell in many places at once without you or your crafts needing to be physically present in any of them.

The Internet has opened thousands of entrepreneurial opportunities on a frontier that seems to have no boundaries. Individuals with a keen sense of what's possible, commingled with large doses of technological savvy, self-confidence, and charisma, strived to meet the challenges offered by the virtual frontier. Some ventures succeeded while others failed. A few of the major ecommerce sites are discussed in this section. For a list of other sites, see the appendix.

Amazon

Among the early pioneers—and biggest success stories—is Amazon. Amazon came online in 1995 as a book retailer, but through steady growth fueled by the acquisition of talented individuals and other, smaller dot-com businesses, it now claims to be the largest online retailer in the world, with books just part of its expanding inventory. True, crafts can be found for sale here, but this may not be the best place to present your handmade work. Because shoppers tend to use Amazon to look for the best deals, you may be at a disadvantage, as dozens upon dozens of crafts importers use Amazon as a storefront or fulfillment service.

Like most businesses, Amazon generally makes money off every item it sells. If you sell fewer than forty items per month through an individual account, you will be charged 99 cents, plus a number of other variable fees, per sale. If you expect to sell more than forty items per month, you can set up a professional account for $39.99 a month plus fees. How well you can expect to do on Amazon depends on what you have to offer and your price points. One-of-a-kind items are difficult at best to sell on Amazon. Production items may be more successful.

If selling your work on or through Amazon isn't viable for your crafts business, the company has other services worth mentioning. With Amazon Webstore, which has monthly fees ranging from $25 to $55 a month plus selling fees, you can set up your own ecommerce site within the Amazon system. You can even point your own domain to your webstore. Amazon also offers a payment solution called Checkout by Amazon, which you can set up on your own website and that allows your customers to purchase items using their Amazon account information. To learn more about how to sell on Amazon, visit the website, scroll to the bottom of the page, click on the "Sell on Amazon" link, and explore the various services offered.

eBay

eBay also came online in 1995 as a place to auction collectibles. Today most things legal can be either auctioned or sold for a flat fee through the company's Buy It Now system. Like Amazon, eBay may not be the best place to sell one-of-a-kind items. People have to find the item first, and with millions of things for sale, the chances of several people discovering yours and getting into a bidding war are slim. Also as with Amazon, you will have to pay a number of variable fees for items you sell on eBay. Monetary transactions are handled through PayPal, which also charges a fee for each item, and you will need an account here as well.

Etsy

Neither Amazon nor eBay is designed exclusively for crafters, and therefore buyers have millions of items other than crafts to sort through. Etsy, on the other hand, is an ecommerce website almost exclusively for handmade items created by you. I say "almost exclusively" because two other categories of goods can be sold on the site: vintage items of twenty or more years old and supplies for crafters. Etsy charges a 20 cent listing fee per item, plus a 3.5 percent sales fee when sold. Listings expire after four months and then must be renewed.

With Etsy, you set up your own shop with photographs, descriptions, prices, and other information about your merchandise and yourself. You can also choose your preferred method of payment: PayPal, check, bank transfer, and so on. Buyers purchase directly from you, not from Etsy. You fill the orders and ship them.

Etsy has an active forum where shop owners can ask questions and get advice. According the April 2012 Etsy "Weather Report," found on the forum, $63.6 million of goods were sold by the community, up nearly 68 percent from April 2011 sales. Is Etsy a good place for *you* to make money on your crafts? That depends on what you're selling and how well you present it. Other factors also come into play. Some people do very well, as statistics indicate, but others apparently do not, according to statements made on the forums. You can explore the forums to get an idea of what others are doing.

Blogging and Social Networking

The personal blog (short for web log—that is, diary) has been around in one form or another since the late 1990s. Active blogging is a great way to get to know people—virtually, at least—and become known. The emphasis here is on "active." This means posting to your blog at regular and frequent intervals and regularly commenting on others' blogs. Posting regularly gives people a reason to return to your site, and commenting shows your interest in someone else—who in turn will likely show interest in you.

This begs the obvious question, What do you blog about? After all, we're talking about marketing and selling crafts, not your summer vacation. And blogs you follow and comment on will in some way be relevant to your craft or crafts in general.

Your blog should be an adjunct to your business website, and the content you provide should in some way be meaningful to your market. Write about your current projects and products, upcoming events you'll be participating in, your experiences with past events, and anything else relevant that you think of. One of the functions of all this activity is to create fresh content for search engines to find, which in turn helps push your site higher in the search rankings. Your posts should have lots of *keywords* related to your craft, which are words that people use when searching for information. This is part of a strategy called *search engine optimization* (SEO). The more people you have visiting your site, the greater the chances of your becoming known as an expert or someone with desirable products. You and your business become *brands* that people recognize.

Networking through social media is now a mainstay of the Internet community, and it's hard to imagine that there is anyone who has not heard of Facebook, YouTube, and LinkedIn, to name three prominent social media sites. Each of these sites, along with dozens of others, has a different focus and function. Facebook, which allows people to keep in touch with friends and family, also has a Pages feature specifically designed for businesses as a means to keep connected with their customers. On YouTube, the video repository owned by Google, you can upload videos about yourself and your crafts. LinkedIn is a business site where users can network with other professionals, post résumés, seek employment opportunities, and find employees or contractors to work with.

One thing all social media have in common is interactivity. This ongoing interaction with colleagues and customers further reinforces your brand and your reputation.

Marketing Online: The Bottom Line

Although it may be possible to have a viable crafts business without at least a modest Internet presence, your chances of success increase the more you get involved in marketing online. But therein lies a problem. Maintaining a website, writing content for your blog, following and commenting on other blogs, updating your status on Facebook, creating videos for YouTube, tweeting your activities on Twitter, maintaining your connections on LinkedIn, and updating your Etsy shop all take an enormous amount of time. Never mind that you are working within a structure that is filled with alluring distractions that can bring productivity to a screeching halt.

Making the Internet work for you takes time, enormous self-discipline, and at least some technical know-how. You also will benefit from a reasonable strategy and schedule for the time you spend online versus in your shop or studio. After all, you are in the business of making crafts. You need to spend some time doing what you love to do.

chapter 7

Service, Fulfillment, and Sales Reps: Keeping Your Customers Satisfied

Whether you sell only at weekend street fairs, in galleries, at trade shows, or exclusively online, each customer has a specific need. Do you know what it is? Do you know what your customers or potential customers *really* want? Well, they want the same thing you do: to be happy and satisfied. Satisfaction comes when a problem is solved. I'm not necessarily talking about a problem in the negative sense; I'm talking about the problem of fulfilling basic human needs.

Some people are shopping for crafts because they are looking for just the right gift. Others are because they want something special for themselves. When you provide what your customers want and need, you are helping them solve a problem. Seen this way, you also are providing a service.

It's said that you can do everything wrong in business and still succeed if you provide good customer service, and conversely, you can do everything right and still fail if you provide poor service.

Customer Service

The term *customer service* may bring thoughts of long waits on hold on the telephone, after responding to several prompts to press this number or that, and hearing repeatedly how important your business is and "thank you for your patience."

As an independent sole proprietor of a crafts business, especially if all your sales are one-off, you may not give customer service a second thought. Yet service begins the moment buyer and seller greet one another. Providing good service simply means treating your customers well, even if it's only in a ninety-second exchange.

Quality merchandise is the first criterion for good service, because without great and well-crafted products, you won't have many customers. But if anything does go wrong with one of your creations, you'll want to help your customer solve this problem quickly. How you do that depends on the situation, but first you must be easy to find.

When handling customer complaints or problems, listen attentively and patiently. Give feedback to indicate you've understood the problem as stated. This will clear up any misunderstanding or miscommunication. Next, offer the best solution available, replacing the item at your cost if appropriate. Whatever the solution, follow through as soon as possible.

Depending on your business model, you may have three different categories of customers: those who buy directly from you at retail events, those who order from you through your website at retail, and wholesale accounts such as galleries and shops. The kinds of service and solutions you offer will depend on the customer category.

Perhaps a wholesale customer is having trouble selling a particular item and wants to return stock to you, even if you've stipulated all sales are final. Why not offer an exchange? It doesn't hurt to ask, and it could lead to new designs and ideas for other products.

Good service means keeping the customer satisfied. Guaranteed satisfaction guarantees future business.

Fulfillment and Shipping

Fulfillment, in general, means coming through with what you promise, whether it's helping with a problem, standing behind a warranty or guarantee, or promptly filling an order. If you sell in any way other than directly, where you do not exchange cash for crafts across the table, you'll be involved in filling orders. To fill an order, you package your products and ship them to your customers.

The principle ways of sending products from one place to another are via the US Postal Service (USPS), United Parcel Service (UPS), and Federal Express (FedEx). Large, palletized shipments go by motor carrier, or commercial freight. Depending on your business, and what and how much you ship, you may eventually use all of these.

The USPS offers two basic ways of mailing items: Parcel Post and Priority Mail. Parcel Post is a standard delivery service, and delivery time varies according to distance. Delivery of Priority Mail items is generally faster, usually within two or three days of shipping. The costs of both modes are based on weight, with Priority generally being the more expensive of the two. This is assuming that you use your own packaging. The USPS offers a variety of specially marked Flat Rate boxes and envelopes usable only for Priority shipping. Prices range from $5.15 to $15.45 as of this writing. Flat Rate boxes have a generous weight allowance, so in some cases it may be much less expensive to use a Flat Rate box instead of your own packaging for a shipment of the same weight. You can also order Regional Rate boxes in several different sizes from the USPS website; depending on the distance between your zip code and that of the customer, these can be an even less expensive option.

UPS and FedEx also offer ground services with costs based on weight and delivery zone. Package size may also be a pricing factor; a small package of the same weight as a large one may be less expensive.

With the USPS, UPS, and FedEx, you can establish an online account whereby you can pay postage or shipping fees and create shipping labels. The USPS offers a discount for postage purchased on its website or on eBay. You can also buy US postage from several online services (see the appendix).

A tracking number and delivery confirmation are important if a delivery dispute arises with one of your shipments. These are included in the cost of FedEx and UPS shipments. With the USPS, delivery confirmation with a tracking number is often included for free or at a significant discount when purchasing online postage, depending on the method of shipment, but incurs a relatively large additional charge when purchased at the post office counter. All three services offer expedited and overnight shipping at significantly higher prices.

The USPS offers Priority Mail Flat Rate boxes and envelopes, as well as Regional Rate boxes, free of charge, but if you use another shipping method or service, you'll need to obtain your own boxes, not to mention other supplies. See the appendix for a list of shipping supply houses that offer volume discounts for boxes and other necessities.

If you're shipping a relatively large order, such as five or more thirty-pound boxes or a full trade-show exhibit, you may find it less expensive to ship via common carrier, also known as motor carrier or motor freight. For the trucking industry, this kind of order is relatively small, considering that many semitrailers are packed with goods from large manufacturers and suppliers bound for huge retail outlets and factories. But these small shipments are so common they have their own category called less-than-truckload (LTL) shipping.

The charges for shipping via common carrier are highly variable and complicated, but don't let this deter you from using this mode when appropriate. Though the best advice on LTL shipping can be obtained from local freight companies, including FedEx and UPS, here are a few terms and conditions that are useful to know.

A *tariff* is a book that lists a variety of rate schedules and options. Tariff sometimes also refers to the rate itself. The *chargeable weight* is, as the name implies, the weight at which you are charged. It is not necessarily the actual weight of your shipment, however. For example, you may be charged by volume *in the van*, which has a predetermined weight assigned to it. The charge to you is based on the greater of weight or volume. The *break point* is that point at which it is less expensive to ship in a greater weight category, since rates begin to drop as weights increase. Weight rates are listed in units per hundred pounds, for which the term is *centum weight* (*cwt*), or hundredweight. *Point to point* refers to rates based on shipping between two major cities. *Mileage* rates are based on distances between nonmajor points, whether origin, destination, or both.

When writing an order, buyer and seller must understand exactly what the shipping arrangements are. How will the goods be shipped? Who pays for shipment? Who owns the goods and is responsible for them during transit? How will the transfer be handled? The answers to these questions should be spelled out on the order form. The shipping industry uses the term *free on board* or *freight on board* (*FOB*) to make certain distinctions regarding the shipment. FOB is followed by either a point of origin or a destination. Who holds title to the goods and when and where that title is transferred are indicated by the FOB designation.

Let's say your studio is in Portland, Oregon, and you are shipping to a gallery in Cleveland. *FOB factory* means that the buyer arranges and pays for shipping from your door and is responsible for the goods from the moment the order is picked up for shipment. *FOB destination* is just the opposite: you make the arrangements, pay the costs, and own the goods until they arrive at the gallery. *FOB Portland* or *FOB shipping point* means that the buyer takes responsibility once the goods are delivered to a specified point of departure other than your studio—a trucking company loading dock, perhaps. You pay any *drayage* (short trip) charges to get the merchandise to the trucking company. *FOB Cleveland* is just the opposite. *FOB destination, charges reversed* means that you own and are responsible for the goods until they arrive at the gallery, but the buyer pays the shipping costs. *FOB factory, freight prepaid* means that the buyer owns the goods and is responsible for them as they come from your shop, but you pay the shipping costs.

The consideration of ownership is most important in case of damage in transit. Who deals with the carrier if there is a claim? If the buyer owns the goods from the moment they are shipped, then he makes the claim against the shipping company. That is the only way he will be reimbursed for the goods (unless you agree to replace them gratis with salable merchandise). Then he can reorder if necessary. If you own the products until they arrive at the gallery, then the dispute is between you and the carrier. You are still obligated to fill the order.

Sometimes these shipping designations are open to interpretation, so be sure to clarify anything that isn't perfectly clear.

Also, when putting together an order, always include a *packing list* or *manifest* in each box of the shipment. This list should include all items within the box or total shipment and indicate whether each box is part of a larger collection of boxes, for example, box four of five.

Sales Representatives

Larger manufacturing operations employ sales forces to call on potential buyers. As salaried or commissioned personnel, they represent a direct cost to the company. The independent crafter has no need for, and indeed cannot afford, a sales force of any size. Smaller businesses, crafts included, have created a niche for another kind of entrepreneur: the sales representative. Also called a manufacturers' rep or sales agent, the sales rep works hard making a good living selling your items and the items of others strictly on a commission basis of 15 to 20 percent of wholesale. The more he sells, the more he makes.

If you are having no trouble selling what you make and can make a living at it, a rep is unnecessary. But if you're looking to expand into new territory, or you haven't the time or inclination to be on the road selling much of the time, a rep may be just the person you're looking for. What's nice about having a sales rep is that he does the legwork while you concentrate on your craft. The sales rep will make routine calls on your regular wholesale customers to ensure they have plenty of your crafts in stock.

Many sales reps come to trade shows or advertise there, looking for clients. They also advertise in trade publications. Sales reps, who usually work in territories, have dozens of contacts. They generally build their lines with noncompeting products. Because they make their living at selling, they are selective about what they add to their collection, avoiding products they don't believe they can sell. Sales reps also can work certain shows for you, but not all. Some show promoters require that the crafter and his assistants attend the booth.

The crafter's job is to provide the rep with sample products and sales literature. The rep does not buy these products. The rep's job is to seek orders and turn them over to the crafter, who has the responsibility of fulfilling all the other duties incumbent on the sale: packing, shipping, billing. Because the rep is paid only after you are paid, it is in the rep's best interest to ensure the buyer's creditworthiness.

As your agent, the sales rep represents you to buyers you may or may not know personally. What he says and does reflects directly on you and your business. Also, as your agent, the rep has the power to sign sales contracts to which you are legally bound. A rep can tie you up financially by filling your production schedule at the expense of your other clients. He also might place items in outlets where you may not want them. Though these are extreme cases, such problems can happen. It is to your advantage to be scrupulous when selecting a sales rep.

One or more good sales representatives can be a boon to your business, provided you establish the proper working relationship. Your sales rep should know as much about your product as you do. It isn't fair to ask him to be like you, but you can expect him to represent you in a manner acceptable to you. Because he also has a reputation to maintain, the sales rep should work *for* you and not against you. At the same time, you have a responsibility to make the rep's job as easy as possible with good product support and customer service. If you can't meet an order deadline, let the rep know so that he doesn't walk unaware into an embarrassing situation the next time he pays a call on a retailer. And as a matter of professional courtesy, do not compete with your representative by selling directly to retailers he has established and cultivated.

The Itinerant Crafter: A Booth for the Crafts Nomad, Indoors and Out

Selling crafts on the road is a nomad's life. As a nomad, you need to carry your shop with you. And whether an event is indoors or out, you need to be prepared for a variety of circumstances.

For outdoor events, the first thing you need is a portable canopy. The typical size is ten by ten feet. The canopy demarks your space and protects you and your goods from the elements. Canopies range in quality and price. You can expect to pay anywhere from $200 to $1,000 for a canopy plus a variety of extras, including a wheeled case and side panels. If you're going to do more than a couple events in a year, get the best-quality canopy you can afford.

Canopies come in two main parts: the frame and the top. The frame is either aluminum or steel. Aluminum frames, which are more expensive than steel ones, are lighter than steel but not as strong. Some lightweight frames may be too flimsy to withstand moderate wind. Frames may consist of components that need to be assembled on-site or may be collapsible with telescoping corner posts.

Choose a frame with vertical corner posts. Many of the lighter-weight canopy kits add stability by angling the posts outward, thus reducing the interior space. This also limits your ability to add side panels if necessary.

Tops are made of polyester canvas. Canvas weight is measured in *denier*, with 500 denier (D) being the standard weight for tops. Most commercially available canvas tops are water resistant and flame retardant. Although canvas may be available in many colors, it's best to buy white because this may be a requirement for some events.

Side and back panels are an additional expense, but they are valuable in the long term. Panels further define your territory. They keep people from wandering into the booth from behind or the side and offer greater protection from the elements.

The roof configuration of your canopy is also important. The flatter the roof, the more chance it will collect water. Even peaked roofs may collect water around the edges. Rounded roofs are less susceptible to water collection.

A slight breeze can be an annoyance at any event, but a heavy gust of wind can ruin your day. Experienced crafters use fifty or sixty pounds of weight at each corner when wind is expected. You can purchase commercially available canvas bags to hold sand or gravel and attach them with Velcro straps to the corner posts. One trick is to hang gallon jugs filled with water from the framework. Five-gallon jugs used for camping work well, too. Water-filled containers offer the advantage of easy portability when they are empty, assuming you have a water supply on-site.

You may wonder why experienced crafters use weights rather than stakes to secure their canopies against wind. First, many events are set up on asphalt or concrete. Stakes will not work there. But what about parks and other grassy areas where many events are held? In most public areas, stakes are prohibited for safety reasons. Left behind or in the ground, they pose a danger for people at play and a hazard for lawnmowers.

Another consideration when choosing a canopy is ease of setup and takedown. The crafts community is a helpful one, and you can usually find someone to lend a hand, but sometimes you may be on your own. After you've acquired your new canopy, put it up and take it down a few times to ensure you've got the hang of it. Setup at a retail event can be a rushed affair, and it's important to know the snags you may face before you plunge in.

Finally, you need a means to cart your canopy from your vehicle to the site. A wheeled case may be included in the package or may be an extra. It's a good thing to have either way.

Lightweight and rugged folding tables come in several sizes, and you'll likely want at least one. A folding chair, and perhaps a second for an assistant or guest, is also a must. A small toolbox that includes pliers, duct tape, clear tape, scissors, utility knife, and a selection of bungee cords is a valuable asset. After you've done a few shows, you'll know better what extras you will or won't need.

Maintain a special container for all your promotional and sales materials, including business cards, order forms, brochures, and laminated newspaper and magazine clippings about you and your work for visitors to browse through.

Other things you need in your booth depend on what you have for sale. Will you need clothing racks, folding shelves for pottery, or tabletop racks for jewelry? Are you a minimalist or do you wish to liven up your booth with banners and drapery? Keep in mind, however, that the more things you assemble in your booth, the more you'll have to manage before and after the event.

Indoor events don't require a canopy to protect you and your merchandise from the elements, but you'll still need everything that would go inside the booth. As with an outdoor booth, your indoor setup depends on what you have to offer and how you'll display it. Freestanding panels and shelving are available from companies like Armstrong Products (see the appendix), but you can make your own with a little ingenuity. You may want to use special lighting to enhance your display. If so, account for this when you design your booth, but first find out if electricity can be supplied to your booth. There may be an extra charge for electricity. As always, your booth should be a compromise among durability, portability, and efficiency.

Whether your display sits outdoors under a canopy or inside at a trade show, it can take one of two basic configurations: closed or open. Closed configurations have a table along the front of the booth, separating you from shoppers. Your inventory is on the table, available for inspection. While this gives you good oversight of your merchandise, it also creates a boundary between you and the buyer. In an open configuration, crafts are displayed on one or more of the side and back walls, with nothing separating your booth from the aisle. Shoppers are automatically welcomed into your space to browse. Which configuration you should use depends on what you have to offer and your personal taste. Experiment with several arrangements to find the one that works best for you.

chapter 9

On Paper: The Back Office of the Crafts Business

Next to undercapitalization, poor management kills more businesses than any other ailment. Effective business management requires good communication and leadership skills, whether it's working with customers, employees, or business partners. For some, this comes naturally; for others, it can be an obstacle. Programs like Toastmasters International provide great opportunities for learning communication and leadership skills. But perhaps even more important, good business management also requires proper accounting and record keeping.

Although computers and accounting software have taken most of the paper out of paperwork, accounting and record keeping continue to vex many small-business owners who can't afford to hire someone to take care of these niggling but necessary details. But even though you'd rather be working on your craft, you can't ignore these details if your business is to survive.

This chapter deals with the importance of developing and maintaining good business skills, the behind-the-scenes work necessary to keep your crafts business afloat and on course through the doldrums of slow months and the rapids of fast ones.

Planning for Success

Few mariners would set sail without charts to guide them. Businesspeople, too, need charts. One of those charts is the business plan. Some business plans are elaborate documents outlining the history of the company, its products and services, management personnel, sales goals, competition, financial standing, and other pertinent details. Companies use the plan as a tool for acquiring capital from outside sources. The crafter, however, has little use for such a complex plan. For your purposes, a business plan serves as a way to consolidate your thoughts. It is analogous to working through a new design. The fiber artist makes a sketch, perhaps dozens of them, before beginning to weave. The furniture maker first draws a detailed set of plans from which to work.

Unless you are seeking financing to start or expand your business, no one but you needs see your business plan. Indeed, if you seek financing, potential lenders will require a business plan. It's their main source of information about your business when evaluating their investment risk. Nevertheless, it's important to get in writing exactly what you mean to accomplish and how. Putting your plan in writing converts a vague idea into a workable form.

A good business plan includes a *mission statement* as well as a *financial forecast*, which gives you an idea of where you should be, or hope to be, over time. A one-year forecast is typical, but you can plan for longer periods as well. The three most useful parts of the forecast are the *income and expense analysis*, *break-even analysis*, and *cash-flow analysis*.

Mission Possible

Begin your business plan with your mission statement. Your mission is what you do, not what you hope to accomplish sometime in the future. Even if you haven't yet started selling your crafts, it's important to see yourself operating a successful business. Use your mission statement as a reminder to help keep you from getting sidetracked and as a source of inspiration. Your mission statement should indicate your market, your contribution to the market, and what distinguishes you from others. Here is a sample mission statement: "Providing high-quality wooden boxes for people who appreciate fine handicrafts at a reasonable price."

Income and Expense Analysis

An income and expense analysis, figured as accurately as possible, is essential because it gives you a year-end income goal to shoot for. It helps you decide where you want to be, or where you can expect to be, financially at the end of the forecast period. You tally your potential expenses for the year and match them against potential income. The difference is either net profit or loss. To turn a loss into a profit, you must either cut costs or increase sales, or both.

Every business has two categories of costs: fixed costs and variable costs. *Fixed costs* are those incurred by the business itself. They include studio or shop rent, salaries (yours and other executives'), taxes, and expenses for utilities, machinery, repairs, maintenance, general advertising, trade shows, travel, bookkeeping, and legal services. Other fixed costs to consider are interest on loans and depreciation on equipment. Depreciation takes into account the reduction in value of an item over time and allows for the eventual replacement of equipment. Fixed costs, then, are those expenses not associated with production; they are the collective costs of operating the business. Calling them "fixed" costs may be misleading. No cost is truly fixed for long. Indeed, many fixed costs fluctuate widely.

Distinct from fixed costs are *variable costs*, which are those directly associated with production. They include the costs of materials and labor (employees). Variable costs rise and fall along with production. The more you produce, the more materials and labor you have to put into the process. Also included in variable costs are commissions paid to sales representatives, who are paid per unit, and some advertising costs, when they apply to specific products.

If you've been in business for a while, you already have an idea of what your fixed costs will be during a given year. If you're just starting out, you must rely more on estimates than on actual figures. In any event, think of as many fixed costs for the following year as you can, list them, and apply a dollar amount to each one. Next, determine how much money you expect the business to earn that year. You should have an idea of both the quantity of goods you can produce and the income you can expect to derive from sales. The determination may be largely speculative, but it should be as realistic as possible. The income and expense analysis, then, should answer the following question: "Do I have a reasonable chance of making any money during the upcoming year?"

Break-Even Analysis

The second part of the forecast, the break-even analysis, tells you exactly at what level of production you will meet your costs. This is the break-even point. When sales go above this point, you realize a profit. When sales do not reach the break-even point, you have a loss.

To do a break-even analysis, you need three pieces of information: fixed costs over one year, variable costs per unit, and price per unit. Let's assume a total fixed cost of $30,000, variable costs of $15 per unit, and a per-unit price of $25. This example is based on the production of one product only. When more than one product is involved, the variable costs and price

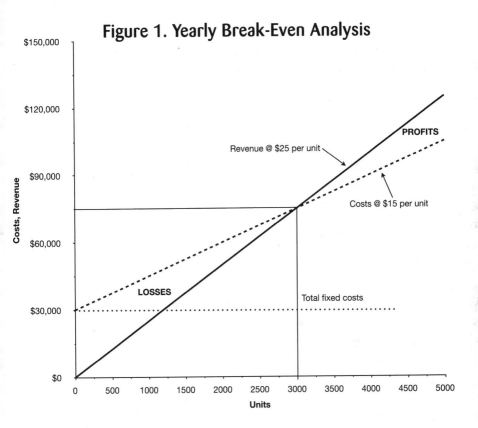

Figure 1. Yearly Break-Even Analysis

per unit would each be an average of all products. Alternatively, you can do a break-even analysis for each product.

The break-even analysis is easily set up on a spreadsheet, and then illustrated on a graph. The horizontal x-axis at the bottom represents units produced. The vertical y-axis to the left represents both costs and revenue. The horizontal line drawn at $30,000 represents fixed costs.

To establish the costs line, multiply each unit increment by $15, and add to the result the $30,000 fixed cost. To establish the revenue line, multiply each unit increment by $25. The two lines converge at the break-even point. Note that on the graph in Figure 1, the break-even point is the production (and sale) of three thousand units, with a total cost and a yield of $75,000.

Notice that until the break-even point is reached, the $10 difference between the unit cost and the unit price is not profit; it represents the contribution each piece makes toward the fixed costs. Profit occurs only when sales surpass the break-even point.

Cash-Flow Analysis

All businesses have their ups and downs, their good months and bad. The crafts business is no different. It can be a feast-or-famine proposition. A month-by-month cash-flow analysis can help you even out the peaks and valleys. *Cash flow* is the term used to describe cash coming in and going out. A negative cash flow means that more goes out than comes in at a given time. This, of course, is not good. The cash-flow analysis pinpoints those months with positive and negative cash flows. You are in a better position if you plan to use money earned during the fat months to help tide you over during the lean ones.

The difficulty when you're just getting started is that you have no idea which months you need to watch out for. To be accurate, cash-flow projections need to be based on past performance rather than educated estimates. Once you have a year's worth of business behind you, you'll have the necessary data to begin. Tally each month's expenses and sales, then look for a pattern. Chances are the pattern reflects the major trade-show periods of summer and winter. Whatever the pattern, use the information as an aid in making cash flow work for you.

Pricing for Profit

Determining the price of a handcrafted object—whether it's a production item or one of a kind—often can be a muddled affair, full of puzzles and variables. Some variables are more under your control than others. All of them represent, in one way or another, costs of doing business. Accurate pricing requires continual and meticulous record keeping of both time and costs. It also requires a healthy knowledge of the market and its trends, plus a strong dose of good judgment.

This section deals primarily with how to determine wholesale prices for your wares. But because the wholesale price ultimately determines the retail price, crafters who sell exclusively at the retail level will also find the information useful. Unless specified otherwise, *price* in this section refers to wholesale price.

The price of any item, what a retail merchant will pay to own it, is made up of three components: *fixed costs*, or *overhead*; *variable costs*, or *direct costs*; and *profit*. *Fixed costs*, as discussed above, are the expenses of the business itself. Theoretically, these costs never change, especially over the short term. Though they allow production to take place, fixed costs are separate from variable costs. *Variable costs*, the actual expense of producing crafts, are the costs of wages and materials, and these fluctuate depending on how much or how little is produced.

Profit is what you or your company makes after your costs have been paid for in sales. If you plan for your business to make a specific profit each year, then consider this as one of your fixed costs and include it in your calculations. If you want each product to earn a specific amount of profit, then include it as a variable cost in your calculations or add it later to a predetermined base price. Regardless of how you figure it, profit is what your business earns for itself. In the following discussion, profit is *not* considered a cost or included in the calculations.

There are two basic approaches to setting price. The cost-plus method involves working from the bottom up. You set a price based on the cost of producing one item—or a specific number of items—plus a profit. The second method, the market-based approach, starts at the top, with the price fixed at a point where you believe maximum profit can be achieved. You then attempt to bring costs in line with the price. Both methods assume relatively stable costs and continual production. Neither should be used without regard for the other. If cost-plus pricing yields a price too high relative to the market, business may suffer with a loss of sales. If costs are ill considered in market-based pricing, profits may erode quickly if they are used to subsidize production.

Determining Costs

You price, however you determine it, can be represented as a formula. A formula is a concise way of expressing a concept and illustrating a conclusion: $a + b + c = d$. The formula itself is not so important as the fundamentals and principles behind it. And it's crucial, from a business standpoint, to get a firm grasp of your costs and what you need to charge to cover them.

Because making crafts is a way of life as well as a means to an end, it may seem confining and overly bureaucratic to apply a rigid formula to pricing the products of your free-flowing imagination. The crafter with an understanding of these fundamentals and principles, and the ability to apply them, has an advantage in the marketplace. This said, we first need to determine the values of a, b, and c in an effort to determine d—the price.

The a in the formula represents the *fixed costs*. The section on doing an income and expense analysis above provided some explanation on what they are, but some further elaboration may be helpful here.

A salary is a fixed amount paid to you or others at scheduled intervals. Wages are variable costs paid to you or your *production* employees for work done, whether by the hour or by the piece. Wages paid to a bookkeeper or other *nonproduction* employees, however, are fixed costs. As a crafter with a business, you take on a number of roles, such as designer, handicrafter, mechanic, secretary, and bookkeeper. How you pay yourself, whether by a salary, a different wage for each job, or a combination of both, is up to you. But be reasonable. Deciding that you will pay yourself $100,000 a year right off the bat may not be the best move for your business. In reality, crafters often earn much less than minimum wage on a per-hour basis. A forty-hour week is something vague, impractical, and possibly even too short for your purposes.

Whether you work in your basement, garage, or someplace away from your home, your next costs to consider are those connected directly with the workplace. If you work outside the home, overhead costs are straightforward; you know exactly what they are because you pay bills each month. If you work at home, however, figuring these costs takes a little more time and effort. First, measure the total square footage of your home, including the studio or shop. Then measure the square footage of your workspace alone. Divide the workspace figure by the home figure to determine the percentage occupied by the workspace. Then multiply the other costs of operating your home that are common to the business—utilities, insurance, mortgage or rent—by this percentage and allocate these costs to the business. For tax purposes, discussed later, you can add to your percentage the square feet used to store merchandise if it's not already included in your workspace calculations.

Total your yearly fixed costs, and then break them down into a more manageable unit, such as a month, week, or day. Let's assume your total fixed cost for one week is $600.

The *b* in the formula represents the variable costs. Let's say you make jewelry boxes of wood. You have on hand a supply of different hardwoods, a bolt of blue velvet for lining, and a box of hinges and catches. The objective is first to determine the cost of the material going into *each* box. This involves straightforward calculations based on your costs for materials: the price of lumber per board foot multiplied by the number of board feet per unit, plus the cost of hardware and other parts. Let's assume a materials cost of $4 per unit.

The next step is to determine how much labor is involved per unit. This is not as straightforward as calculating unit materials costs because there are so many variables. But for the sake of setting up a workable production model, you will have to make some other assumptions.

Say you can make twenty-five boxes in one week, but to do so you need a part-time assistant whom you pay $12 an hour for twenty hours' work. In one week, your materials cost $100 and your labor costs $240. Although your labor cost may seem fixed, it's a variable cost because it's tied to production. Some weeks you may make only twenty boxes, other weeks you may make thirty, all for the same labor cost. But labor cost *per unit* will vary accordingly.

In the example here, the weekly variable costs come to $340. The materials cost per box is $4, the labor cost per box is $9.60 ($240 ÷ 25), and the unit variable cost is $13.60 ($9.60 + $4).

Cost-Plus Pricing

The cost-plus method of pricing provides a visual model of costs at any point of production. As an analytical tool, it enables you to break down and apply a cost per unit based on a specific number of units made. The goal of this analysis is to help you establish a base price at which all of your costs are covered. This model uses seven costs to help you analyze production status at a given time. The first two, total fixed costs for one week ($600) and unit variable costs ($13.60), have already been explained. The other five are unit fixed cost, total variable cost, total cost, unit cost, and marginal cost.

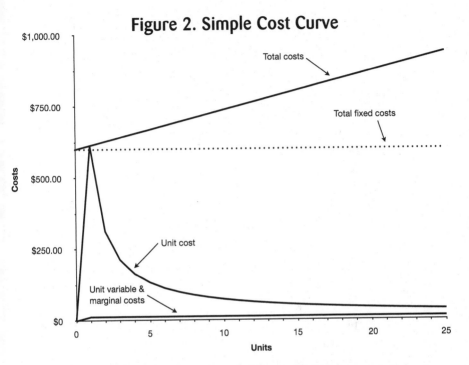

Figure 2. Simple Cost Curve

Unit fixed cost is the portion of the total fixed costs incurred by each of a specific number of items. This cost decreases by quantity produced. It illustrates how each unit contributes to the coverage of total fixed costs. If you make only one item during the week, then your unit fixed cost is $600. If you make your projected twenty-five boxes during the week, then the unit fixed cost (at optimal production) is $24 ($600 ÷ 25).

Total variable cost is the accumulated unit variable costs as production increases. If a single unit costs $13.60 to make, then two units cost $27.20, and so on. Thus the total variable cost is $340 ($13.60 × 25).

Total cost is the sum of the total fixed costs and the total variable costs. Here the total cost is $940 ($600 + $340).

Unit cost is the total cost of each unit as it's produced. Dividing the total cost by the quantity derives the unit cost. Your

Table 1. Data for Simple Cost Analysis

A	B	C	D	E	F	G	H
Quantity	Total fixed cost	Unit fixed cost tfc ÷ q	Total variable cost	Unit variable cost tvc ÷ q	Total cost tfc + tvc	Marginal cost	Unit cost tc ÷ q
0	$600.00	$0.00	$0.00	$0.00	$600.00	$0.00	$0.00
1	600	600.00	13.60	13.60	613.60	13.60	613.60
2	600	300.00	27.20	13.60	627.20	13.60	313.60
3	600	200.00	40.80	13.60	640.80	13.60	213.60
4	600	150.00	54.40	13.60	654.40	13.60	163.60
5	600	120.00	68.00	13.60	668.00	13.60	133.60
6	600	100.00	81.60	13.60	681.60	13.60	113.60
7	600	85.71	95.20	13.60	695.20	13.60	99.31
8	600	75.00	108.80	13.60	708.80	13.60	88.60
9	600	66.67	122.40	13.60	722.40	13.60	80.27
10	600	60.00	136.00	13.60	736.00	13.60	73.60
11	600	54.55	149.60	13.60	749.60	13.60	68.15
12	600	50.00	163.20	13.60	763.20	13.60	63.60
13	600	46.15	176.80	13.60	776.80	13.60	59.75
14	600	42.86	190.40	13.60	790.40	13.60	56.46
15	600	40.00	204.00	13.60	804.00	13.60	53.60
16	600	37.50	217.60	13.60	817.60	13.60	51.10
17	600	35.29	231.20	13.60	831.20	13.60	48.89
18	600	33.33	244.80	13.60	844.80	13.60	46.93
19	600	31.58	258.40	13.60	858.40	13.60	45.18
20	600	30.00	272.00	13.60	872.00	13.60	43.60
21	600	28.57	285.60	13.60	885.60	13.60	42.17
22	600	27.27	299.20	13.60	899.20	13.60	40.87
23	600	26.09	312.80	13.60	912.80	13.60	39.69
24	600	25.00	326.40	13.60	926.40	13.60	38.60
25	600	24.00	340.00	13.60	940.00	13.60	37.60

price point—that is, the price you set for the finished product—*must* be at or greater than your unit cost for you to at least break even. In this example, the unit cost for twenty-five boxes produced is $37.60 ($940 ÷ 25).

Marginal cost is the cost of producing one more unit. For example, the total cost of producing fifteen units is $804 and of sixteen units is $817.60.

The marginal cost is $13.60. Note that as long as the total variable cost rises in even increments, the unit variable cost and the marginal cost remain constant. Table 1 depicts these costs for one week's production of twenty-five units. Figure 2 illustrates the unit cost, unit variable costs, total fixed costs, and total costs based on the data in the table.

At this point, the marginal cost—which in Figure 2 follows the same course as the unit variable cost—may seem irrelevant. That's because, in this scenario, fixed costs and variable costs are unchanging and production is steady at an optimum level; it's a "perfect world" picture. Realistically, however, fixed costs do change over time, and variable costs are almost never constant. Many factors can be attributed to fluctuating variable costs.

Let's say you've designed a new box you want to put into production. Essentially, the first box you make is one of a kind, so production is slow and well below optimum level. Your variable cost therefore is much higher, especially in labor. Also, there may be a greater-than-average waste of material. Keep in mind, however, that as overall production increases, you will buy more material. A volume discount will decrease your per-unit cost.

As you learn the most efficient way to cut and assemble the pieces that go into the box, production increases to the optimum level. But chances are it won't stay there. Production slows when fatigue sets in and machinery needs attention. An unexpected contributor to a slowdown can be too much production. What do you do with all of those boxes, complete and incomplete, as they pile up around the shop hampering your progress? And eventually you'll have to stop and sweep the floor.

The next table and set of graphs illustrate another hypothetical yet more realistic picture. Table 2 includes all the data used to create Figures 3 and 4. Amounts for the total variable costs are arbitrary (as variable costs will be) for this illustration, but all other amounts are calculated according to their specific formulas. Unit fixed costs and marginal costs are excluded from Figure 3 for clarity. Figure 4 zooms in on the unit variable costs and shows other costs in relation to them.

Notice in Table 2 and Figure 4 that the unit variable costs and the marginal costs are high at the beginning of the production run but begin to drop as efficiency improves. Production reaches the optimum level at the tenth unit, when the unit variable cost approaches its previously established level of $13.60. Also notice the drop in the marginal cost. At optimum production, the marginal cost levels off, while the unit variable cost continues to fall. At the seventeenth unit, the marginal cost begins to rise (again, for a variety of hypothetical reasons). Even though the variable costs are still on the decline, the cost of producing the seventeenth unit is greater than the cost of producing the sixteenth. Although the unit variable cost is increasing, it's still below $13.60, your established cost at optimal production. Your costs are still covered, however, because your marginal cost (the cost of producing one more unit) is still less than your unit cost. This remains the case through the twenty-fourth unit.

But look at the costs for number twenty-five. The cost to make the twenty-fifth piece is greater than the unit cost. As the unit variable cost rises, so does the marginal cost. When the marginal cost moves above the average cost per unit, the unit variable cost begins to increase faster than the unit fixed cost decreases. It costs you more to make item twenty-five ($45) than you can sell it for at its assigned unit cost ($40.72).

Table 2. Data for Realistic Costs Analysis

A	B	C	D	E	F	G	H
Quantity	Total fixed cost	Unit fixed cost tfc ÷ q	Total variable cost	Unit variable cost tvc ÷ q	Total cost tfc + tvc	Marginal cost	Unit cost tc ÷ q
0	$600.00	$0.00	$0.00	$0.00	$600.00	$0.00	$0.00
1	600.00	600.00	20.00	20.00	620.00	20.00	620.00
2	600.00	300.00	38.00	19.00	638.00	18.00	319.00
3	600.00	200.00	55.00	18.33	655.00	17.00	218.33
4	600.00	150.00	71.00	17.75	671.00	16.00	167.75
5	600.00	120.00	85.00	17.00	685.00	14.00	137.00
6	600.00	100.00	97.00	16.17	697.00	12.00	116.17
7	600.00	85.71	109.00	15.57	709.00	12.00	101.29
8	600.00	75.00	120.00	15.00	720.00	11.00	90.00
9	600.00	66.67	130.00	14.44	730.00	10.00	81.11
10	600.00	60.00	139.00	13.90	739.00	9.00	73.90
11	600.00	54.55	148.00	13.45	748.00	9.00	68.00
12	600.00	50.00	157.00	13.08	757.00	9.00	63.08
13	600.00	46.15	166.00	12.77	766.00	9.00	58.92
14	600.00	42.86	175.00	12.50	775.00	9.00	55.36
15	600.00	40.00	184.00	12.27	784.00	9.00	52.27
16	600.00	37.50	193.00	12.06	793.00	9.00	49.56
17	600.00	35.29	203.00	11.94	803.00	10.00	47.24
18	600.00	33.33	218.00	12.11	818.00	15.00	45.44
19	600.00	31.58	238.00	12.53	838.00	20.00	44.11
20	600.00	30.00	260.00	13.00	860.00	22.00	43.00
21	600.00	28.57	283.00	13.48	883.00	23.00	42.05
22	600.00	27.27	308.00	14.00	908.00	25.00	41.27
23	600.00	26.09	338.00	14.70	938.00	30.00	40.78
24	600.00	25.00	373.00	15.54	973.00	35.00	40.54
25	600.00	24.00	418.00	16.72	1,018.00	45.00	40.72

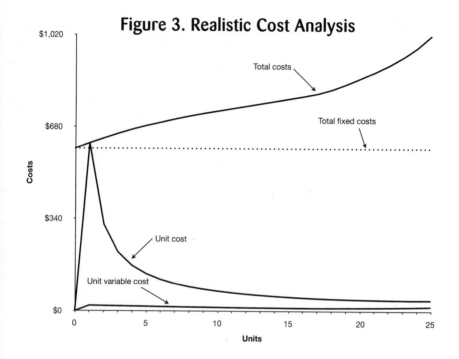

Figure 3. Realistic Cost Analysis

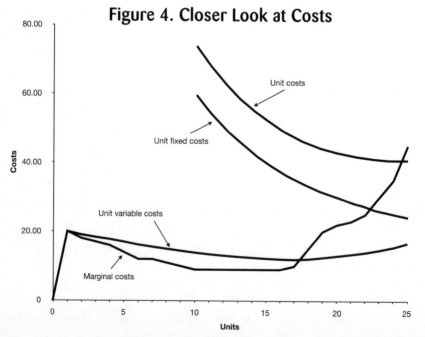

Figure 4. Closer Look at Costs

Once you've established your price point based on unit cost, you then can add the desired profit, *c* in the formula, to set your wholesale price, *d*. This done, the percentage of the markup can be applied to other items. Remember, though, that you can add profit as either a fixed cost or a variable cost at the beginning of the process rather than tack it on at the end.

In a perfect world, where costs, demand, production, and sales remain constant, cost-plus pricing is ideal. Few crafters, however, work in a perfect world. Costs do fluctuate. And you can never be completely sure of demand. Critics of cost-plus pricing argue that the method largely ignores market demand in its calculations.

When used by itself for pricing production work, and with total disregard for the market, the cost-plus method is risky. For commissioned work or high-end, one-of-a-kind work where demand is nil until the piece is finished, it is far more practical. The value of the cost-plus model of setting price is twofold. First, it forces you to think in terms of costs. Second, it allows you to see exactly how these costs are affected by the vagaries of production.

Break-Even Analysis Revisited

The break-even analysis enables you to see the point where revenues equal costs at a specific production level and at a given price. Items sold at a price above this point yield a profit, below this point, a loss. Used in conjunction with the cost-plus model, it helps you set a realistic price and better manage your production schedule.

As with the cost-plus method, the break-even analysis makes several major assumptions: first, that you sell everything you make at the price you ask; second, that fixed costs remain static and total variable costs increase at an equal per-unit rate; and third, that you can accurately estimate demand at various

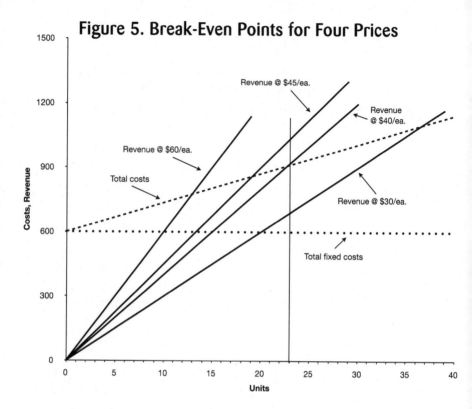

Figure 5. Break-Even Points for Four Prices

prices. These assumptions point out the weaknesses of the analysis. Under conditions of widely fluctuating costs, the value of the break-even analysis is diminished because it tends to distort and oversimplify reality.

Using our established figures of $600 a week in fixed costs and a constant unit variable cost of $13.60 as used in the simple cost analysis, Table 3 shows the break-even point for four base prices. At $30, you would have to produce thirty-seven boxes in a week's time to cover costs. At that price, each box would contribute $16.40 to your total fixed costs ($30 – $13.60 in unit variable costs = $16.40). At $60 you would have to produce just thirteen boxes a week, and each one would contribute $46.40 to overhead costs.

Table 3. Break-even Points for Four Base Prices

Price point	Unit variable cost	Unit contribution to TFC (pp-uvc)	Total cost at break-even point	Units needed to break even	Revenue at break-even point
$30.00	$13.60	$16.40	$1,103.20	37	$1,110.00
40.00	13.60	26.40	912.80	23	920.00
45.00	13.60	31.40	872.00	20	900.00
60.00	13.60	46.40	776.80	13	780.00

The $30 price is far too low because, in our scenario, producing thirty-seven boxes a week is not possible without hiring more help, which would increase your costs. At $60, production strain is eased. It is unlikely, however, that you can sell many of your thirteen boxes at that price. A $40 price point more closely fits the desired price of $37.60 established in the cost-plus analysis, and you need only produce twenty-three units to break even. Figure 5 shows the break-even points for the four prices shown in the table.

Market-Based Pricing

The cost-plus method of pricing builds a price from the bottom up. The other extreme is working from the top down, basing price on current market conditions. This form is useful when facing fierce competition and a traditional expected price range exists. This method makes the important assumption that once you've set a market-based price, you can then tailor your costs to fit within the range.

Suppose your wooden box competes with several others of similar nature and quality in the $40 wholesale range. Suppose further that your costs demand that you set your wholesale price at $60. Your choices are either to maintain your price at

$60 or to reduce it to within the expected range. If you stick with the first option, you can expect to sell fewer boxes than your competition, if any. If you choose the second option, it's imperative that you pare your costs to make up for the lower price.

The objective of market-based pricing is to determine a price at which maximum profit can be realized. The first step is to determine demand at various price points.

If you can sell six items at $60, your yield is $360. But suppose you can sell eight items at $50. Your yield then would be $400. Twelve items at $40, the competitive market price, is $480. Perhaps if you cut your price below your competitors', you will be able to sell more items and therefore make up the difference in volume.

Other Considerations

Thus far, pricing has been discussed in terms of formulas. Pricing formulas, whether based on costs or the market, are merely tools for the crafter and work best when used together with a dose of good judgment. Now is the time to depart from such rigidity, gather stray thoughts, and tie up loose ends.

Striving for profit over the long term has more benefit for the crafter than seeking short-term profits and sales for the sake of sales. It is acceptable, and sometimes wise, to take a loss on some items. The goal is maximum profit on the combined output rather than on each unit.

Ultimately, you set your price to reflect the work you put into the piece as well as its other costs. The more competitive the item, the more the price has to be in line with the market. If it is truly unique, you likely will be able to demand a higher price. At the same time, so can your dealer. Don't be surprised if you find some items marked up more than 100 percent. Do be surprised, however, if it's less. Retailers who discount your work are underselling your other dealers. This is especially a problem if several dealers in the same area are selling your work.

Wholesalers and retailers view markup differently. The crafter can think in terms of a 100 percent markup on the wholesale price. An item with a wholesale price of $20 will retail at $40. But retailers think in terms of a markup of 50 percent of the retail price: 50 percent of $40 is $20. Both yield the same result, but they arrive at this result differently.

People have a general idea of the value and price range of certain objects. For example, you may expect to pay $800 to $1,200 for a standard refrigerator. If the item were priced higher than the range, it would have to have a greater *apparent* value to justify the price. Adding apparent value with features that *appear* to increase the overall value is a practice that lets manufacturers offer a variety of merchandise at a variety of prices. An item's *brand* may also add apparent value. The apparent value may or may not reflect the actual value and quality. The same holds true for crafts. A buyer of handcrafted work will make a judgment on the expected price of a certain item. If the price is out of that range, the buyer wonders what added value or values justify the increase. One-of-a-kind work is a good example. Its uniqueness automatically increases its value beyond actual costs, especially if a crafter's reputation comes along with the piece.

Having an idea of the expected retail price of any item you produce helps you judge where to set your wholesale price. If the expected price is below your cost of producing the item, then you must somehow increase the product's value or apparent value, or both. You can add new features, place it in outlets where it can be compared to more expensive items, or concentrate on an advertising campaign that will lend it more prestige (branding). If the expected price is above what it costs you to produce the item, you have great leeway to maximize profit.

The crafter actually has to deal with two expected price ranges: wholesale and retail. Since the retailer has an expected range for items in her store, she also has an expected price for crafts purchased at wholesale.

In general, a price should not be lower than expected, because this would project a loss of apparent value. Referring again to the refrigerator, if you expect to pay at least $800 for it but the price tag is $500, you might wonder what corners were cut during its manufacture. A psychological disadvantage also accompanies a price below the expected range. A buyer's ego may prevent her from paying too low a price. And who among us hasn't, at one time or another, purchased a costly item instead of a similar, less expensive one with the belief that the more it costs, the better it must be?

Once wholesale or retail prices are established, stick with them until you see a need to change them. Erratic price changes appear unprofessional. On the other hand, prices are always on trial, and changing them when necessary is no crime. As a rule, it is easier to work with a high initial price within the price range than a low one. If you find you must lower the price, you have the psychological advantage of creating a bargain. On the other hand, raising the price without an increase of apparent value risks the loss of goodwill.

When the Price Is Right: The Potter's Tale

Once upon a time, there was a potter named Ben. Ben had a small business, which he operated out of his garage. He earned a modest living, but no matter how hard he worked, his business never seemed to grow beyond making ends meet. Almost every weekend, he packed his van with pottery and traveled to a crafts fair, sometimes as far away as three hundred miles. Once or twice a month, he took pieces of his best work to a number of gift shops and galleries in his area, placing them on consignment.

One day, while setting up a new account at a gift shop, Ben learned that the owner was preparing to go to a trade show. Ben had heard about trade shows but had never given them much thought. To him, trade shows meant commercialism, something that was worlds apart from the art he produced. The shop owner convinced him that his work was appropriate and would be well received at the show.

Ben decided to give it a try. Eight months later, he found himself in a brightly lighted arena surrounded by pottery buyers from all over the country. He was gratified by how much the buyers liked his work. At the end of the second day, Ben had a nice stack of orders. They felt good in his hand. He said to himself, "I bet there's enough work here to keep me busy for six months, maybe even a year." And he was right. His production time was booked nearly solid. Just after lunch the next day— and with a twinge of regret—he put up a sign on his booth that read, "No More Orders."

That night in his hotel room, he spread out his order sheets and began tallying the receipts. "A year's worth of work," he kept thinking. "I can't believe it." But soon his stomach began to tighten and sweat beaded on his forehead. Something wasn't right. True, he had a year's worth of work. But he did not have a year's worth of income.

For the first time, he thought about his job, his profession, and his craft as a business. He had always wondered why, no matter how hard he worked, he was just barely scraping by. "I just have to make more pots," he'd keep telling himself. But now he saw that he couldn't possibly increase production. He reflected on his days selling at retail fairs, when he could keep the entire price of each piece he sold. He hated cutting his retail price in half for these wholesale buyers. "How can anyone make a living selling at wholesale?" he asked himself. "If only I had all of these orders at retail, I'd be set. But if it's so bad, why do all of these other crafters seem to be doing so well?" Then it hit him—all the while, even when he was just breaking even at retail, he was actually selling at price points that should have been wholesale. Ben was practically giving his work away.

The moral of the story: poor pricing strategies are bad for business.

Let's examine Ben's situation. How merchandise is priced—not knowledge and quality of craft—is perhaps the most important difference between the professional and the amateur crafter. There was nothing wrong with Ben's work, which he executed with skill and finesse. But his prices branded him an amateur, and the buyers took advantage of him. Buyers know how much they can get for a certain piece. In a competitive crafts market, with all things being equal, the retail price is generally set at twice the wholesale price. If a competitively priced bowl wholesales for $20, the gallery owner then retails the piece at $40. Into this setting comes our potter Ben, offering a fine-quality bowl for $10 wholesale. The buyer sees that it's easily worth $40 retail and sells it at that price, which is certainly fair and ethical, because as the legal owner of the piece, she can do anything she wants with it. Another way to look at it is that the potter paid the shop owner $10 to buy his bowl.

Because the amateur is unsure how to set the price, and of the relative value of a given piece, this uncertainty puts him at a disadvantage, rendering him unable to market his crafts adequately. An inexperienced negotiator may even ask the wholesale buyer to set the price, putting both parties in an awkward position. The buyer knows what he can get for your work, but he isn't going to share that information with you.

Low, noncompetitive pricing is one reason professional crafters tend to avoid some retail events, particularly small local fairs and bazaars, where one may find merchandise of lesser quality. Buyers seeking the lower prices here may suspect that sellers with higher, albeit more reasonable, prices are gouging.

The professional crafter prices competitively. The amateur prices randomly, giving little thought to the true costs of production. Often the motivating force of the amateur is merely to generate enough income to replenish his stock of materials so that he can continue with his craft. And that's fine if the amateur is content to operate in a world of amateurs and hobbyists. But as soon as the amateur steps unprepared into the professional world of crafts marketing, he's in trouble.

Professionals understand pricing inside and out, from the top down and the bottom up. They know what they must charge to make a living and what they must not charge to avoid pricing themselves out of the market. In other words, their prices are competitive. The crafter who doesn't have a handle on pricing naively takes a wrecking ball to the competitive structure. This does not mean that crafters actively engage in price fixing. Rather, in a true competitive market, prices tend to stabilize within a certain range, dictated by demand.

Let's look at the potter's tale from a different perspective to see how unrealistic pricing can hurt not only the amateur's business, but the businesses of other crafters as well. Our potter, skilled though he is at his craft, is naive about how to set his prices. At his first trade show, he offers price points that attract a horde of buyers who enthusiastically place order after order. He realizes that if he continues to take orders, he will be unable to meet the obligations. Reluctantly, he stops taking orders, even though the show has one more day to run. He tallies his orders and estimates the income he expects to realize from what appeared to be an unbelievably successful first show. After subtracting his estimated production costs, however, he realizes that he will barely break even. The show was not such a success after all.

Also at the show were four veteran trade-show sellers offering wares similar to those of our friend, at prices about 30 percent higher. Their experience, though, was just the opposite of the amateur's. Because so many buyers scooped up merchandise at the lower prices offered by the amateur, the veterans saw a reduction in orders for their own more realistically priced pottery.

This is a recurring problem for many professional crafters. Although they know that the amateur who undercuts the market—and himself—will likely be out of business in a couple years, it is little consolation; there will always be someone else to fill the niche. And today many American crafters also must compete with foreign importers offering mass-produced knockoffs at much lower prices. For buyers looking to save money, even "Handcrafted in America" may not outweigh a bargain.

Basic Business Structures

Every business must have a base of operation. The facilities you need often dictate where you locate this base, and where you locate has an impact on your expenses. Many crafters are able to work right out of their homes. This works for you in two ways. First, it reduces costs, because you already have utilities in place and will have no additional rent or mortgage payment on another place. Second, you get to take advantage of the tax deductions the Internal Revenue Service (IRS) offers to those who operate businesses in their homes (more on this later). By working at home, you save money, which is another way of earning money. Imagine the pressure of having to earn an extra $1,000 a month just to pay shop expenses. This way, if you do earn that extra grand, it goes into your pocket, not someone else's. Don't discount the possible need to expand into larger quarters as your business grows, however. Another advantage to working at home is the time saved in travel. And as the saying goes, time is money. You save on meals, too, if you don't eat out.

Whether you work in your home or at another location, you are expected to comply with a host of regulations. Are there any zoning restrictions in your area? Will you need any special licenses or permits? Answers to such questions can be found on the local and state levels, but specific governing agencies vary from state to state. All state and local governing agencies have websites where you'll likely find all the information you need, or you can make some phone calls to local government offices at city hall or the county courthouse.

All businesses in the United States fall into one of four organizational structures: proprietorships, partnerships, corporations, and limited liability companies. Each has its own liability and tax implications, which you should carefully consider.

Proprietorships

The *proprietorship*, or sole proprietorship, is the simplest form of organization and the easiest to start. In it, you (and, if you choose, your spouse) are the sole owner of the business, and you work for yourself. You personally assume all the risks and liabilities involved in doing business. All personal assets are commingled with all business assets, and there is no legal distinction between the two. You (or your estate) are personally liable for any debts incurred by the business or claims made against it.

All business income is claimed on your personal tax return, Form 1040, with profit and loss calculated on Schedule C. Self-employment taxes, which pay into social security, are calculated on Schedule SE. You are required to estimate and pay income taxes quarterly, accompanied by Form 1040-ES.

Whether you need to register with a particular state agency varies from state to state. You may be required to file an assumed business name if you operate under any name other than your own.

Partnerships

The *partnership* is similar to the proprietorship, except two or more people are involved. A partnership is simply an agreement between two or more people or parties (a corporation, for example, can be a partner) to do business for profit. Each partner has the ability to act on behalf of the partnership, and all partners are bound by any such activities. All liabilities and other claims against the partnership are shared among the partners; for example, creditors can seize the personal property of all partners to pay off debts.

A limited partnership is a variation on the theme. Limited partners can invest in and share in the wealth of the business but are liable only to the extent of their investment. They are restricted from having an active role in the day-to-day affairs of the business, leaving that to the general partners. If a limited partner assumes an active role in the business, she also assumes the role of general partner, thereby losing limited liability.

Corporations and Limited Liability Companies

The *corporation* is an entity unto itself, separate and distinct from its officers. Each corporation must have at least two officers, a president and a secretary, who also can be shareholders. If you organize your business as a corporation, you are no longer self-employed; you are an employee of the company. The company, then, must assume all the obligations incumbent on an employer, including withholding and depositing income and other taxes from its employees—even if you are the only employee. Your company must file a tax return separate from your own.

As the owner of a corporation, you have a double tax obligation. Your company pays taxes before dividends are disbursed, and you pay taxes on your personal income, including those same company dividends. The IRS has made a provision to ease the burden of double taxation on small corporations, called S corporations, where income is taxed only once at the shareholder level.

Corporations offer liability protection, which is one of the things that make them attractive. For example, creditors can seize only company assets, not those of its officers or shareholders; therefore, your personal estate is protected.

Two disadvantages of a corporation are the complexity of paperwork and the necessity to withhold and deposit payroll taxes of employees. Yet another form of business entity, the *limited liability company* (LLC), offers liability protection without the burden of payroll taxes. There are two kinds of LLCs: *single-member* and *multimember*. The single-member LLC is similar to a sole proprietorship in that you account for your business income and expenses on your personal Form 1040, Schedule C. Tax returns for multimember LLCs are more complex, but the idea is the same: liability protection without the burdens imposed on corporations.

To help ensure protection against liability, always transact company business under the auspices of the corporation or LLC. When you sign a document, make sure you indicate your official capacity in the following manner: Roland Monk, President, Monkeyshines Crafts, LLC. Avoid conducting company business as an individual or handling personal affairs under the company name. This muddies up your bookkeeping, which, in turn, can become a problem if the IRS ever audits you.

Business Requirements

Each state has stringent rules dictating what is required for the organization and operation of a partnership, corporation, or LLC, including filing specific documents, writing annual reports, holding annual meetings, and perhaps even issuing stock. Because of the legal and tax ramifications, it is wise to seek legal advice before filing any papers.

If you operate your business under any entity other than a sole proprietorship *or* you have one or more employees, you will need a federal tax ID number, known as an employer identification number (EIN). See the IRS website under Businesses for details.

For further advice on business matters, contact your district office of the Small Business Administration or visit the SBA website. This federal agency, established in 1953 to promote the cause of small businesses, disseminates valuable information and advice on all manner of business-related topics. Furthermore, the SBA puts the Service Corps of Retired Executives (SCORE) at your service. This is an organization of retired businesspeople whose volunteer members are available for consultation.

See the appendix for contact information related to the above business entities and taxation.

By the Books

When you begin a crafts business, you will realize that the most important thing needed to sustain it is constant sales. This is fundamental to any business, and no business can survive long without steady revenue. A sale is simply the exchange of goods or services for dollars. The more exchanges, the more dollars. And that means growth.

Or does it? It does when the increase in dollars outpaces the increase in expenses. It doesn't when expenses keep pace with or outpace income. It's impossible to gauge a business's growth (or lack of growth) by bank deposits alone, because these give you only part of the picture. You need to look at the entire picture.

To see the whole picture, you need to keep good records. This doesn't mean making sure you put every slip of paper—receipt, invoice, check stub, or what have you—into a large paper sack for an accountant to figure out later. It means properly keeping track of all those transactions for your accountant (or you) to figure out later.

It may be useful to make a distinction between bookkeeper and accountant. The bookkeeper's job, clerical in nature, is to record transactions in the checking, savings, and other accounts. The bookkeeper may also pay bills, submit invoices, and do other routine financial duties. The accountant, who has a college degree in accounting, plays a more analytical role. The accountant compiles reports and makes projections and recommendations based on records kept by the bookkeeper. A given company may employ one or more of each. An employed accountant may be the person to fill out and submit the company's tax returns. A certified public accountant (CPA) is licensed by the state to do accounting for individuals and corporations.

Most likely, you will be your own bookkeeper *and* your own accountant. Fortunately, business accounting software makes bookkeeping and accounting relatively easy. (See the appendix for a list of software providers.) I say relatively easy, because you still need to set up your accounts carefully and be scrupulous about keeping good records for the software to be of any real use. It's advisable to talk to an accountant or consultant *before* purchasing software and setting up your accounts. This may save you money and many hours of frustration.

If your business is small and uncomplicated, and it stays that way, you may not need an accountant—except, perhaps, to complete your tax returns. But what is small and uncomplicated to one person might be large and bewildering to another. And what about when things change, when your business grows? As things get more complex, you are bound to have more and more questions only an accountant can answer, especially about taxes and payroll. An accountant can spot potential problems, ones you may not see, and point out ways to correct them. What's more, an accountant can figure the quarterly reports and financial statements necessary for obtaining financing.

What an accountant can do for you relates directly to the information you give him. If, when it comes time to do your tax return, you turn over to your accountant a boxful of receipts, bank statements, invoices, and all the other various slips of paper associated with your business, you will make the accountant's job more time-consuming—which may cost you.

Adequately kept books do one more thing besides telling you the state of your business: they represent you well to the Internal Revenue Service. If you are audited and your records are sketchy, the IRS may disallow some perfectly legitimate deductions on the basis of lack of substantiation. The IRS is very particular about such things as your income and the deductions you claim. Well-kept books—with the receipts, invoices, and vouchers to back them up—will work to your advantage if you are ever audited.

Another advantage of having an accountant is that he can represent you to the IRS in case of an audit. The costs of consulting with an accountant and an attorney before you embark on a business venture will be much less than hiring them to get you out of a fix later on.

Checking Accounts

Even though paper checks are used less and less frequently, checking accounts still serve an important function for your business. They are a means of keeping separate your business and personal lives. When you are someone's employee, all money you bring home is personal income. When you work for yourself, all income still is personal, but the IRS wants you to make a distinction between business and nonbusiness uses of your money. This is easiest done with two checking accounts: one for business and one for personal, nonbusiness transactions.

When you work for yourself as a sole proprietor or single-member LLC, you neither make wages nor earn a salary. When you pay yourself—that is, take money from the business for personal use—you take what is called a *draw*.

Money spent on business expenses can be listed as a deduction on your tax return; draws can't because they are personal and not business related. If you must pay business expenses out of personal funds, don't pay the expense from your personal account. Instead, write a check from your personal account and deposit it into your business account as "personal funds contributed" or similar designation.

Employees

When you hire one or more employees, another complex set of bookkeeping chores becomes part of the regimen. You are responsible for withholding federal and state income taxes, social security (FICA) taxes, and workers' compensation and unemployment insurance premiums. All of these withholdings must be remitted regularly to the proper agency. Social security and workers' compensation require equal contributions by the employer and the employee. In other words, the employee pays half of the obligation and you pay the other half.

Wages paid to your spouse or children are deductible expenses. You must, however, follow the same procedures as you would with hired employees, including issuing W-2 forms and withholding taxes. Children under age eighteen are exempt from social security and Medicare taxes, and they are exempt from federal and state income taxes if they are eligible to claim exempt status on Form W-4. A word of caution applies: wages paid to family members and used as a deductible expense must be physically paid and, preferably, kept apart from your personal account. For example, a check drawn on your business account and given to your spouse as deductible wages shouldn't be deposited directly into your joint checking account. You are, in effect, taking a draw *and* a deduction.

If you plan to hire employees, you will need to file Form SS-4 (or apply online at the IRS website) to acquire an employer ID number (EIN). For specific information on withholdings and state and federal regulations regarding employees, or to obtain tax tables and remittance forms, contact both the IRS and your state's revenue department.

Sales Taxes

Only five states do not collect sales taxes: Alaska, Delaware, Montana, New Hampshire, and Oregon. If you live in any state other than these, you're obligated to collect, and pay, sales tax on retail sales made within your state. Each state has its own rules, rates, and procedures, so be sure to check on them before you start selling. Where I live, in Washington, the Department of Revenue holds regular regional sales-tax workshops for new business owners.

Petty Cash

A petty cash fund is an easy way to take care of small, day-to-day expenses that come up in all businesses. A petty cash fund is easy to maintain, provided all receipts are accounted for and only one person is in charge of the fund. To start a petty cash fund, simply withdraw a fixed amount of money, say $50, from the bank and place the cash in a box or an envelope. When you need to make a cash purchase, the cash is readily available. The important thing to remember is when you remove money, replace it with a receipt for the goods or services bought, and return any change to the fund. This way the fund always balances: the cash and receipts always represent the total value of $50 in the fund. When the fund gets low on cash, tally the receipts and write another check for the exact amount to refurbish the fund. Record the transactions, then store the receipts.

Invoicing and Following Up on Wholesale Transactions

When you sell directly to the consumer, the transaction is *usually* complete when money is exchanged for merchandise. I say usually because of the possibility of a dissatisfied customer or some other reason you may have to revisit the transaction. In wholesale transactions, you may be extending credit to the buyer. When you ship merchandise on credit, always include an invoice instead of sending it later. Unless otherwise specified, payment is due upon receipt of the goods. An invoice contains the same information as the order: names and addresses, terms, shipping data, damage claim conditions and limitations, quantity, description, and prices of merchandise, and the grand total. The invoice should also include a serial number for reference. The difference between the invoice and the packing list is that the invoice is a bill. It is official notification that you wish to be paid under the agreed-upon terms.

File a duplicate copy of the invoice in an accounts receivable file until it is paid. In a perfect world, you will receive your money within thirty to forty-five days. In a less-than-perfect world, you may have to ask again to be paid. Each month, review your accounts receivable to see which accounts are overdue. Note these accounts and promptly resubmit a bill with a polite reminder. If you haven't received payment within fifteen days of a second billing, once again resubmit, this time with a slightly sterner reminder. How long you wish to continue billing is up to you, but keep in mind that the longer a bill goes unpaid, the more difficult it is to collect. If an account is more than sixty days past due, consider turning it over to a collection agency. An agency charges you a percentage, but at least you get something for your effort. Before making such a drastic move, however, warn the customer with a letter or email. It may inspire prompt payment.

All businesses are different for the simple reason that all businesses are run by different people. True, all businesses must adhere to certain minimum standards as far as operation and record keeping, but what happens after that is entirely up to the operators of the business. As far as bookkeeping is concerned, the simplest system that covers all the bases is all that is necessary. Which bases you need to cover depends on the size and complexity of the business. The most important thing to remember about keeping track of money is to carefully record where it comes from and where it goes.

With or without computers and accounting software, keeping records is a tedious, time-consuming process that requires dedication and consistency to make it work effectively. IRS considerations aside, adequate record keeping can tell you many things about the state of your business. It gives you an ongoing picture of where you stand as far as income and expenses. It's better to know about problems as they arise than to wind up with a year-end surprise. And because you are constantly aware of your financial standing, you can take steps to minimize problems. Sales mean nothing if they are not ahead of expenses. No business can operate at a loss for long. If you don't know where the money goes—and how much of it is going—you have no idea where costs can be cut.

The Taxman and You

"In this world nothing is certain but death and taxes," Benjamin Franklin said. Indeed, taxes are so much a part of life that many business decisions are based solely on the resulting tax implications. Regardless of what you think of Uncle Sam's taxing powers, all of us must share annually with the government certain information to establish our tax liabilities. We share our information on a sheaf of paperwork known as Form 1040.

The tax system is set up in such a way that profit-seeking businesses are taxed on gains rather than total income. Built into the system are ways by which taxpayers can offset or reduce overall gains and thus reduce their tax liability. Sometimes these are called deductions; other times they are called loopholes. The goal of the IRS is to collect as much in taxes as it can. The goal of the taxpayer is to take advantage of as many (legal) deductions as possible to pay as little tax as possible. The IRS makes a habit of reviewing tax returns to see whether taxpayers are playing by the rules. In general, the IRS will not point out deductions you could have taken, but it will inform you of deductions you shouldn't have taken. And you may be required to pay more in taxes and perhaps penalties, too.

The IRS allows you to deduct reasonable business-related expenses to offset your income from that business. It even allows you to use a business loss to offset gains from another source. A *loss* is when you spend more money on your business than the business brings in. For self-employed people, including single-member LLCs, profit or loss shows up on Schedule C, "Profit or Loss from Business," and is reported on Form 1040.

Note: The information provided in this section is general and should not be taken as tax advice. Bear in mind also that tax laws are always changing from one year to the next.

Home Sweet Studio

Working at home is one of the delightful aspects of being self-employed. There's no commute, it's convenient, you can work when you please, and you don't have to face the world on those days when you don't—or the world doesn't—feel so rosy. What's more, it's a good way to keep costs down. And there are a handful of tax deductions you can take that otherwise would be unavailable.

The IRS, however, has a stringent set of rules that anyone operating a business from the home, including crafters, must follow in order to qualify for the deductions. Foremost, the portion of your home, or outbuilding on your property, used for business must be used exclusively and regularly for business. Second, your home studio or shop must be your principal place of business.

If each day after breakfast you spread out your crafts work on the dining room table, the IRS may disallow the deduction. Only if the room you use for your work is set aside for *exclusive* business use on a regular basis would it qualify. What constitutes a "regular basis" is open to interpretation. There is no set minimum number of hours or days magically separating regular from incidental or occasional. The stipulation that your home be your principal place of business should not be much of a problem. Because of the nature of the crafts business, either you work at home or you don't. There may be some exceptions. If you have a shop in town and sometimes bring work home as a matter of convenience, work you could just as easily do at the shop, any deductions you take would be open to question. This rule applies more to a professional—an attorney, for example, who has an office away from home but reads legal briefs and law books in his den each evening. No home-use deductions would be allowed in this case.

Your crafts business need not be your sole source of income for your home to qualify as your principal place of business. You can have another job and operate your crafts business at home and still qualify. Principal place of business refers to the business in question.

Assuming your home qualifies, you figure your deductions the same way you determined costs of home-business use in previous analyses. Determine what percentage of space you use for your business, and multiply that by the overall costs that apply. You can deduct allocable portions of mortgage interest, property taxes, rent, utilities, depreciation, repair, and maintenance. A word of caution: if you deduct the allocable portions of mortgage interest and property taxes on Schedule C, you may only deduct the remaining portions on Schedule A, "Itemized Deductions." You may fully deduct expenses that are exclusive to your workplace. In all cases, the deductions must be "reasonable."

Expenses for business use of your home are figured on Form 8829 and transferred to Schedule C. For a detailed explanation of whether you qualify and how to figure the deduction for business use of your home, see IRS Publication 587.

The IRS will not allow you to use home-use deductions to create or increase a loss and thereby reduce taxable income from other sources. Those deductions are limited to your net income and cannot cause the net income to drop below zero. First you must reduce your gross income by expenses excluding those for your home studio. Only then can you begin deducting expenses for your home studio and in the following order: interest and taxes, operating expenses, and depreciation. If and when you reach zero, you must stop. You can, however, carry over unused deductions to the next year. One more point: because you can fully itemize mortgage interest and property taxes on Schedule A, you needn't bother with them on Schedule C unless it's more advantageous to do so. An accountant can give you the best advice on this matter.

The Hobby Loss Limitation Rule

The IRS is skeptical of people who year after year claim losses from a business that is supposed to be profitable. The taxman begins to wonder whether such people are truly engaged in business with the intent of making a profit, or if they are merely engaged in a hobby, which may be fun but is no more a business than taking a hike.

Nearly all income, including income from a hobby, is taxable. The IRS has nothing against hobbies even if they earn money, so it allows you to negate that income with expenses incurred in pursuit of your hobby. But to ensure that hobbyists don't take undue advantage of business deductions, the IRS established the hobby loss limitation rule. The IRS will not allow you to take a loss on your hobby. In other words, you may deduct hobby expenses only up to the amount of your hobby income.

What's more, if you are a hobbyist (or a businessperson deemed by the IRS to be a hobbyist), you may not use Schedule C. Income from a hobby is reported on Form 1040 as "other income." Your personal deductions are claimed on Schedule A as "miscellaneous deductions."

By now you may be wondering, "What's all this have to do with me? I'm not a hobbyist; I'm a businessperson. I have a legitimate crafts business." These are good points, and the above discussion on hobbies may have little or nothing to do with you. But it could have more to do with you than you think.

The IRS is interested in your intention of making a profit. It presumes that if you are in business, profit is your intention, not garnering write-offs to offset other income. The IRS has established two tests to help determine whether that venture is a hobby or a business. One of these is the objective "three years out of five" test. If you, as the sole proprietor of a crafts business, realized a profit in three of the last five years, then there is at least the presumption of intent to make a profit. If you pass this test and the IRS still questions your intent to make a profit, it is up to the IRS to prove a lack of intent.

If you fail the test, you have two choices. You can amend previous years' returns to reflect profits rather than losses and pay any taxes and penalties owed. Or you can attempt to prove intent to make a profit by the subjective second test of "facts and circumstances." The IRS has established nine determining factors against which your profit intent is measured. All nine factors listed below are considered together, and no one of them is conclusive.

1. Do you carry out the affairs of your business in a businesslike manner? Do you make use of generally accepted accounting methods? Do you have written contracts with clients?

2. What expertise and training do you have? Do you have any credentials? Have you won any awards for your work? Do you read books and trade journals related to your craft and to the crafts trade in general? Do you consult regularly with an accountant or an attorney about your business?

3. How much time and effort do you put into your business? Do you work on it in your spare time away from another income-producing activity, or did you forsake another activity to pursue your crafts business?

4. How much of an investment have you made in the assets of your business, and do you expect those assets to appreciate? Once you've gained recognition in your field, do

you believe the value of your crafts will increase because of your reputation?

5. Have you been successful in other business ventures?

6. What is the history of receipts and losses of your business? Even though you've failed to make a profit, are receipts increasing and costs decreasing? If not, can you explain increasing losses?

7. What is the relationship between profitable years and years in which you incurred a loss? Can you explain why you had a large loss following a profitable year? If your receipts or profits are merely occasional, how substantial are they as compared with your investment in the business? Small returns for a large investment may indicate a lack of profit motive.

8. What is your financial status? Do you rely on your business income as a necessary supplement to other income, or do you use your business to generate tax benefits for an adequate income from another source?

9. What are your personal motives for carrying out your business activities? Do they deal more with pleasurable or recreational elements rather than with profit motive?

As a crafter, you might have a tough time swallowing the last question. Of course, you take pleasure in your work; that's why you do it. Taking pleasure in your work does not preclude profit motive. But can you demonstrate you are not in business (and taking losses) just for the fun of it?

If, while trying to establish a profitable crafts business, you have incurred losses over several years, your ability to demonstrate intent will figure largely if you are audited.

chapter 10

On Crafts
and Craftsmanship:
True to the Legacy

People have always been drawn to things made by hand. In the past, it was the only way things were made. If you needed a bowl or pouch in which to gather berries, you made one. If you needed a weapon for hunting or defense, you made one. As time passed, some individuals became better than others at making certain things. The family or clan or tribe or village came to depend on these better-skilled craftsmen for the goods they found useful and, eventually, necessary. Skill and knowledge were passed from generation to generation. With skill and knowledge came refinements that increased the apparent value of some items. A knife, for example, was no longer necessarily just a tool for cutting, but it could be a thing of beauty as well. As a thing of beauty, it had aesthetic value. With aesthetic value came pride of ownership.

Not everyone, however, could own an aesthetically pleasing object, no matter how utilitarian. Social status determined who could own what. High status demanded high quality. A distinction emerged between things of purely utilitarian and aesthetic value. But just as status determined who could own things of "quality," it also determined the caste of those who made them. Crafters were workers, crafts a humble occupation. In fact, potters were once among the lowest of the low. Painting and sculpture were considered the only true forms of art.

With the Industrial Revolution, society had less and less need for handcrafted utilitarian goods. A plentiful supply of necessities could now be made one after another by machines and a slew of production workers. Aesthetic value was compromised. No matter; the masses had little need or use for aesthetics. Historically, the less leisure time a given group had, the less interest it had in aesthetics; energy was better spent on survival.

But there always have been those who could afford the work of crafters and artists and had the leisure to enjoy it. And when the nature of crafts transformed from a primarily utilitarian function to one of aesthetic function, buyers of crafts became not consumers but patrons.

In older days, crafters belonged to guilds, which were the academies of craft. Knowledge and skills were closely guarded secrets for the protection of the members of the various trades and of the integrity of the various crafts. Today guilds no longer play the role they once did. And more and more of the masses, now that their energies are not directed solely toward survival, have the ability to buy and enjoy things of quality and beauty.

Pride of owning unique and aesthetically pleasing things made by hand is a powerful motivator. Beautiful things enhance our communal and individual environments and help support our well-being. And few can deny the status involved in owning valuable works of art and craft.

Though guilds have lost their power and function, crafters have not. The contemporary crafter has an unstated obligation, mandated by centuries of tradition, to protect the integrity of his individual craft, and crafts in general, and to pass his knowledge on to capable hands for the continued enjoyment of all.

Despite all the emphasis in this book on business and pro-fessionalism, the inescapable fact is that crafting is foremost a culture, lifestyle, and legacy.

Appendix

The links and other information that follow are for your information only and should not be considered endorsements of any products or services.

Accounting Software
AccountEdge: accountedge.com
Bookkeeper: avanquest.com
QuickBooks: quickbooks.intuit.com
Sage 50: na.sage.com
Simply Accounting (Sage 50 Canadian Edition): na.sage.com /sage-simply-accounting/

Business Plans
Entrepreneur: entrepreneur.com/businessplan
SCORE: score.org
Small Business Administration: sba.gov

Business Structures, Taxes
Visit your state's website for information about forming and registering business entities (Corporation Division) and taxes (Department of Revenue). For local business requirements, visit your city and county websites.
Internal Revenue Service: irs.gov
Limited Liability Company Center: limitedliabilitycompany center.com

SCORE: score.org
Small Business Administration: sba.gov

Canopies, Booths
Armstrong Products: armstrongproducts.com
Canopies by Fred: canopiesbyfred.com
Costco: costco.com
Flourish Canopies & Display Walls: flourish.com

Card Readers, Merchant Accounts, Payment Systems
Authorize: authorize.net
GotMerchant: gotmerchant.com
Imprinters and plates: imprinterplates.com
GoPayment (mobile card reader): gopayment.com
Merchant Warehouse: merchantwarehouse.com
Pay Anywhere (mobile card reader): payanywhere.com
PayPal: paypal.com
PayPal Here (mobile card reader): paypal.com/here
Priority Payment Systems: prioritypaymentsystems.com
ProPay: propay.com
Square (mobile card reader): squareup.com

Crafts Associations
American Craft Council: craftcouncil.org
Craft Retailers and Artists for Tomorrow (CRAFTS):
    craftonline.org
Handmade in America: handmadeinamerica.org

Crafts eCommerce Sites
Amazon
ArtFire, a community of artists selling online: artfire.com
Ebay

Etsy, a place to sell your handmade crafts and vintage items: etsy.com

iCraft, a crafts marketplace in Canada: icraft.ca

Made It Myself, a place to sell crafts and other handmade items: madeitmyself.com

RedBubble, a place to show and sell digital art: redbubble .com

Silkfair, a venue to set up an online store or booth to sell your crafts: silkfair.com

Supermarket, an eclectic blend of crafts and designs: super markethq.com

Wholesale Crafts, a place for retailers to find you: wholesale crafts.com

Domain Name Search Tools

Ajax Whois: ajaxwhois.com

Domain Tools: domaintools.com

Domize: domize.com

NameBoy: nameboy.com

Jury and Application Services

Juried Art Services: juriedartservices.com

ZAPP: zapplication.org

Miscellaneous

Bump contact exchange app for iPhone and Android: bu.mp

Help a Reporter Out (HARO): helpareporter.com

ICANN accredited domain registrars: icann.org/registrar-reports/accredited-list.html

Postage, Shipping

BrownCor: browncor.com

Carton Service: cartononline.com

Endicia: endicia.com
eSupplyStore: esupplystore.com
FedEx: fedex.com
Omnipak: omnipak.com
PartnerShip: partnership.com
Shipping Supply: shippingsupply.com
Stamps.com: stamps.com
Uline: uline.com
United Parcel Service: ups.com
United States Postal Service: usps.com

Publications

Art Fair Source Book: artfairsourcebook.com
Crafts Fair Guide: craftsfairguide.com
The Crafts Report: craftsreport.com

Public Relations, Media Lists

Easy Media List: easymedialist.com
EcommWire: ecommwire.com
Express Press Release: ecommwire.com
Free Press Release: free-press-release.com
The Open Press: theopenpress.com
PR.com: pr.com
PRWeb: prweb.com

QR Codes

BeQrious: beqrious.com
Esponce: esponce.com
GoQR: goqr.me
Kaywa: kaywa.com
QR Stuff: qrstuff.com
Zebra Crossing: zxing.appspot.com

Website Creation Tools (Online)

Drupal: drupal.org
Homestead: homestead.com
Intuit: intuit.com/website-building-software
Joomla: joomla.org
Webs: webs.com
Websites for Etsy Sellers: craftlaunch.com
Weebly: weebly.com
WordPress: wordpress.com

Wholesale Crafts Trade-Show Promoters

American Craft Council: craftcouncil.org
Buyers Market of American Craft: americanmadeshow.com
California Gift Show: californiagiftshow.com
Heritage Markets: heritagemarkets.com
Professional Show Managers Assn.: psmashows.org
The Rosen Group: americancraft.com
Western Exhibitors: weshows.com

Index